LORI PECKHAM, editor

Guide's Greatest

MISCHIEF STORIES

Pacific Press®
Publishing Association

Nampa, Idaho | www.pacificpress.com

Cover design by Steve Lanto
Cover illustration by Marcus Mashburn

The authors assume full responsibility for the accuracy of all facts and quotations as cited in this book.

Unless otherwise noted, Bible texts are from THE HOLY BIBLE, NEW INTERNA-TIONAL VERSION®. Copyright © 1973, 1978, 1984, 2011 by Biblica, Inc.® Used by permission. All rights reserved worldwide.

Scripture quotations marked MEV are taken from the Modern English Version. Copyright © 2014 by Military Bible Association. Used by permission. All rights reserved.

Additional copies of this book are available for purchase by calling toll-free 1-800-765-6955 or by visiting www.AdventistBookCenter.com.

Library of Congress Cataloging-in-Publication Data

Names: Peckham, Lori, editor.
Title: Guide's greatest mischief stories / Lori Peckham, editor.
Other titles: Greatest mischief stories | Guide (Nampa, Idaho)
Description: Nampa, Idaho : Pacific Press Publishing Association, [2019] |
    Selections of true life examples selected from Guide magazine.
Identifiers: LCCN 2019004625 | ISBN 9780816365043 (pbk. : alk. paper)
Subjects: LCSH: Christian life—Juvenile literature. | Malicious
    mischief—Religious aspects—Juvenile literature. | Childrens' stories.
Classification: LCC BV4515.3 .G85 2019 | DDC 242/.62—dc23 LC record
    available at https://lccn.loc.gov/2019004625

January 2019

Contents

A special thanks to the authors we were unable to locate. If anyone can provide knowledge of their current mailing addresses, please relay this information to Lori Peckham, in care of Pacific Press® Publishing Association.

Dedication

To the mischief-maker in all of us.

May this book help us painlessly learn some of the lessons that others had to learn the—*ahem*—hard way.

Acknowledgments

Two competent, caring colleagues (and treasured friends) provided the practical help necessary to complete this book:

Laura Sámano, managing editor of *Guide*, dropped all her other projects to prepare this manuscript.

Melissa Hortemiller, library director at Union College, unlocked the treasures in the college's Heritage Room, welcoming me to explore almost seventy years of *Guide*.

Two creative, storytelling colleagues (and friends) offered inspiration:

Randy Fishell, longtime editor of *Guide*, suggested several of the stories in this volume. (His penchant for mischief also gave him a starring role in one of the stories I found—see chapter 17.)

Mike Mennard, another writing professor at Union College, provided his gift of encouragement. (To tap into some of his crazy creativity, check out mightymagicpants.com.)

> *These six things the Lord hates,*
> > *yes, seven are an abomination to him:*
> > > *a proud look,*
> > > *a lying tongue,*
> > > *and hands that shed innocent blood,*
> > > *a heart that devises wicked imaginations,*
> > > *feet that are swift in running to mischief*
> > (Proverbs 6:16–18, MEV).

1

The Lost Boot Laces

by Ivy R. Doherty

You've got to be faster than greased lightning to catch these grasshoppers!" moaned Don.

He poised his hands on his hips and watched the spot where he thought the grasshopper he'd been chasing had landed in the thick grass. His face, flushed and dewy with the heat of the day, showed signs of the almost hopeless feeling inside him.

Ralph didn't comment. He was too intent on stalking a grasshopper of his own. He took one cautious step, and the dry grass crackled under his shoe. The grasshopper didn't move. Good. Now another step. The dry grass crackled again. The grasshopper didn't move. Very good. Still another step, and still the insect stayed there. Excellent! Two more steps like that, and that grasshopper would surely be in his jar with the others.

But just then Sponge, a neighborhood dog, came bounding toward him and pounced exactly two steps in front of him. The grasshopper fluttered up with a noisy, grinding sound.

"How is it that these hoppers are so lively on such a hot day?" Don complained. "If we have to work as hard as this for bait, how hard do you suppose we'll have to work for the fish?"

Ralph shook his jar and tried to count the catch inside, but there were so many legs and wings mingled together that he gave up. "Tell you what," he said, brightening. "Let's start off with these, and if we need more bait we can catch it later."

"Good idea!" Don agreed.

As they raced for Don's house, where they'd left their fishing poles, Don announced, "Guess what Bud said I could have."

"Not his summer's savings?"

"Ha! Try again."

"No idea," Ralph croaked, trying to catch his breath.

"He said I could borrow his rubber fishing boots."

"Good for Bud! But why is he suddenly being generous?"

Don laughed. "Oh, he's not a bad brother."

"Yeah. Maybe I'm just a little jealous."

"We could take turns wearing them," offered Don. "I'll get the boots and the lunches, and we'll head out."

Ten minutes passed. Ralph looked at his watch impatiently. He couldn't help thinking about the hour or so they'd spent catching those grasshoppers. Finally he yelled out, "What's taking you so long, Don? Get lost in those boots?"

Don sounded impatient too as he explained that he'd found the boots, but the laces were missing. Where could they be? And who would want to take those long laces out of those long boots, just to have to put them back again?

"Come on, Don. Let's fish without the boots," Ralph whined.

"I don't think so," Don argued. "I'll wear these boots if it's the last thing I do." He searched drawers and shelves and closets until his own patience gave way. Finally he helped Ralph gather up the gear, and the two boys took off along the trail at the back of the house.

Don had on the boots. True, they were an awful nuisance without the laces. They bulged open and flopped about. But he was getting to his destination despite the obstacle. And from a distance no one could tell they had only one short piece of string right in the top holes, and that's all. To the onlooker he was now a full-fledged fisherman.

Wagging his tail, Sponge tramped beside the boys. He got his name because he never hunted his food but always expected a handout from someone, just like a sponge.

Soon the boys entered the woods, feeling instant relief from the sun and smelling the pungent earth. Then the steady roar of plunging water met their ears.

"Let's take the first trail that leads toward the falls," Don suggested.

Ferns and sweet-smelling shrubs brushed their legs. Then they spotted their destination through a break in the trees.

Upstream, the river stretched in a long reach of dark, shining water. A fleck of white here and there revealed where a rock hid.

Below were rapids. That accounted for the thundery sound they had heard while still in the woods. Across the river rose a tall mountain, purple and filmy with haze.

The boys looked at each other. Both had the same thought: *This is no place for boys to fish alone.* There were other places, below the rapids, where they could be safe and enjoy all the pleasures of the mountain stream.

Don looked at his boots, then at the green sheet of water that mirrored the mountain.

"They're not going to be a speck of good to you, old pal," Ralph said. "That water will be over your head the very first step you take off the bank."

Don nodded. He knew Ralph was right. Just the same, he wanted to keep them on. They made him feel important, as though he were on official business.

"We'd better go down below the rapids," warned Ralph.

"Look, you're twelve, and so am I," Don replied. "Can't we look after ourselves and not get into any trouble?"

So they took out their gear and the hard-earned bait and cast their fishing poles. They cast again and again, but there was not even the faintest nibble.

Finally Ralph said in disgust, "Let's walk down the riverbank to the quiet place beyond the rapids. Maybe the fish are biting there today."

Don didn't need to be urged. Where there were no fish, there was no fun.

Near the first bend they rounded in the river, they came upon a boat, neat and newly painted, moored close to the bank.

"It must belong to summer people," Don commented. "No one around here owns a boat like that. It really is a beauty, isn't it?"

They dropped their fishing gear and walked all around the vessel. The more the boys talked about and examined the boat, the more they wanted to be in it.

"Wouldn't it be OK if we just got in it and fished a little while?" Ralph asked. "No one would mind if we don't scratch the paint or put bait on the seats."

Don grinned. It would be fun just imagining the boat

belonged to them. In a moment they had stepped in.

As they moved around arranging their tackle, the boat pushed out several feet. That was all the better, they agreed, because now they could cast farther out into the stream than they'd been able to when stuck on shore.

The lines had no sooner hit the water than Ralph gave an excited whoop. He scrambled to land his trout. He pulled and yanked and yelled. But the fish resisted.

Don peered into the water, wanting to catch the first glimpse of the trout's silvery sides. There was a swift shadow and then a flash of silver and finally a terrific splash.

But that splash was no trout. It was Ralph! And Ralph couldn't swim.

"Help!" cried the spluttering form whose head appeared above the water.

"Help!" cried Don, as if he expected a lifeguard to rush to their aid.

Don knew that he was the one who had to help. Quick thoughts flashed through his terrified mind. He'd always boasted about how he could swim, but now Ralph's life depended on him. Could he meet the demand? Overboard he plunged. There was no time to dream about the ifs and buts, for Ralph would soon be carried out of his reach by the current. And what about the rapids ahead?

Don struggled to swim toward Ralph. But what was wrong? His legs wouldn't move. *Ah! The boots!*

He remembered the small string at the top. He ripped wildly at one tie and then at the other. As he kicked furiously, the boots sank to the bottom of the river. He lunged forward, and several sharp, rapid strokes brought him within reach of Ralph.

Ralph grabbed wildly at him, pulling him under the water.

Don came choking to the top. "Don't be stupid!" he gasped. "If you want either or both of us to live, leave me alone—or I'll leave you alone!"

The desperate Ralph clung to Don even harder. Don punched him with his clenched fist. Maybe Ralph could understand that language. He did.

Don wasn't sure how far ahead the rapids were, or whether he was strong enough to pull Ralph to shore before the current swept them farther from shore. While he fought the current, dragging Ralph's heavy body, he prayed for strength. He wouldn't ever tell anybody he could swim well again. This was the real thing, and it was no picnic. His breath came harder and harder.

He tried to remember what to do if the rapids should come before the shore. He would let himself go, trying to keep his arm crooked before his head to protect it from the blows of the rocks. And he would keep the other arm thrust straight ahead so that he could fend himself off from the rocks. This would be all right except for one thing: He had someone else to take care of beside himself, and he just had to get Ralph back home.

His strength was waning. Then his arm touched something rough and cruel. It hurt, but anything hard and substantial to touch was pure joy.

Rock! More rock! Holding Ralph's arm in one hand, Don managed to drag himself onto the rock with the other. He stumbled, exhausted, and then the hammers in his head seemed to pound out a message that he simply could not afford to be exhausted. There was still Ralph to be saved! He pulled and dragged. At last his friend lay limp on the rock. Don dragged him up to a smooth place and set to work, pumping Ralph's back. How he wished Ralph would say something, anything!

Ralph didn't respond. Don realized that he'd have to leave Ralph to get help.

When he raced into his house a few minutes later, his dripping clothes and exhausted look told his mother a great deal—but not enough. "Where's Ralph?" she cried.

"I think he'll be all right. I got him out of the water," he told her.

She grabbed a blanket and hurried to the river with Don.

Ralph opened his eyes as they bent over him. "My head hurts," he moaned. "Why did you hit me, and why am I all wet? Did you knock me into the water?"

"Isn't that what you'd call gratitude?" Don mused to his mother. But he felt so relieved to hear Ralph talk.

Later, just at sunset, Don went back to the boat to find what was left of their gear. There would be no boots to take back to Bud. But what if they had been securely laced? He hated to think what would have happened if they had been. He felt relieved that the laces had been lost. Somehow he felt that maybe God had let them be lost, just to save Ralph's life—and his.

2

The Gravel-Pile Dare

by Paul Burdick

I was always smaller than my playmates. So I ended up getting nicknames, such as "Shorty," "Peewee," and "Runt." I didn't like it. Maybe that's why I looked for ways I could show the other guys that I was as big and strong and smart as any of them.

One of my strategies was to do anything anyone dared me to do. Sometimes it seemed to help the situation, but usually it only got me into trouble.

Soon after my ninth birthday I saved enough money to buy an old, secondhand bicycle. When I got it, it had two flat tires and several other things wrong with it. But with hard work and a lot of help from Dad, I soon had it running.

Much practice and many falls later I could ride quite well. But I still had the same old problem: the bigger boys could ride better and faster than I could. I had to struggle to keep up with them. But there were so many exciting things to do on a bicycle that even though I was smaller, I tried to do everything they did.

One day we stopped to rest for a few minutes by a gravel pile at the bottom of a long hill. The county kept gravel there to repair the roads. There were several truckloads of gravel in the pile, and even though it was spread out, it was still almost four feet high. As we sat on the pile, one of the boys got an idea.

"I wonder what would happen," he said, "if somebody rode down that hill as fast as he could on his bicycle and ran into this gravel pile."

We all knew what happened when a bicycle hit loose gravel. But just what would happen if one hit a whole pile of gravel?

For several minutes we sat there and discussed the idea. Finally the boy who had thought of it began to dare the rest of us to try it. At first some of the boys talked quite seriously about doing so, but when it actually came to starting, they all backed down.

Now here, I thought, *is my chance to prove to them that I'm a lot braver than they are.* So the next thing I knew, I had spoken up and said, "I'll do it!"

At first they thought I was kidding, but as I stood up, picked up my bicycle, and turned to start up the hill, they could see that I meant it. The look of surprise and admiration I saw on their faces was very satisfying.

I proudly rode the quarter mile up the hill. Then at the top I stopped and turned around. It was a long way down! I could see the boys get up from the gravel pile and move to the side of the road, where they stood leaning on their bicycles.

For a moment I wondered if I really wanted to run into that gravel pile after all. But as I remembered the look of admiration on the boys' faces when I had started up the hill, I decided that I just had to do it. After all, I reasoned, the worst thing that could happen would be that I would fall off the bike. And I had done that so many times before that I figured one more time wouldn't be too bad.

I began slowly riding down the hill. Very quickly I picked up speed. Long before I reached the bottom I was going faster than I had ever thought I could!

Still, I kept trying to make the pedals go just a little faster. I could feel the wind whistling past my ears. The gravel pile began to look very large, and I thought once again that maybe I shouldn't be doing this after all. But it was too late to go back.

I gave one last effort to make that bicycle go faster. I was almost to the pile. I saw the boys watching me intently. Then I hit it.

As the front wheel struck the gravel, it twisted to one side and stopped—but I didn't! I left the bicycle, cleared the top of the gravel pile, flew over the barbed-wire fence beyond it, landed in the pasture on the other side of the fence, and rolled over and over on the ground. When I stopped rolling, I wiggled my arms and legs. They worked all right, so I got up and started back toward the fence.

When I had hit the gravel, the front wheel of the bicycle had stopped, but the back end had followed me over the gravel pile and had come to rest leaning against the fence. As I climbed back over the fence and hauled my bicycle to the road, the boys were all talking and laughing. They said that I had put on a good show. When I heard that, I just stood there and grinned.

But it wasn't long before I began to feel something itching and stinging my legs . . . then my arms . . . then my back . . . and my neck. Pretty soon I was itching and stinging all over. All at once I realized what had happened.

In the section of central Tennessee where I lived, many of the fields were covered with small, flat cactus plants that had thousands of tiny spines all over their leaves. I had landed and rolled in one of those cactus patches. Now hundreds and hundreds of those sharp little spines were sticking in my skin!

I didn't say anything about the cactus spines to the boys. But as soon as I could, I told them it was time for me to go and I started home. I hated to tell my mother what had happened, but I was hurting, so there wasn't anything else to do.

She spent most of the rest of that day with a magnifying glass and a pair of tweezers, pulling out cactus spines. When night came there were still many of them left. They were so embedded in my skin that she couldn't get them out, and they began to fester and hurt even worse.

I was so sick I didn't get much sleep that night, and for three days I couldn't go to school. And it was many more days before the sores from those cactus spines went away.

As I lay in bed with my cactus spines those three days, I did a lot of thinking. I thought about bicycles and gravel piles, about pastures and cactus patches. But most of all I thought about dares.

I decided that the next time someone dared me to do something, I would think a little more carefully about the results before I agreed.

3

Who Was the Show-off?

by Maryane G. Myers

It was a risky thing to do. Don Evans knew it before he did it. But the package of firecrackers on his bedroom desk was a greater temptation than he could resist.

Maybe I shouldn't take it to school. But Tom Breeson has been asking for trouble, and he'll get it today, right under his desk! Don told himself.

He slipped the firecrackers into his pocket and hurried outdoors. It was a frosty gray morning, but the thought of Tom jumping with surprise made it seem as balmy as spring.

That show-off will probably yell and really upset things—Miss Caskey's nerves, if nothing else. He laughed at the thought.

Don was still chuckling when he entered his classroom some time later.

Sandra Wilson, who sat at the desk on his left, motioned to him. "Remember the surprise Miss Caskey said she would have for us today?" she whispered.

Don sat down and leaned toward her. "Do you know what it is?"

"I think so. She was talking with another teacher in the hall when I passed a moment ago. I heard her say something about a drawing contest."

Sketching was Don's favorite hobby. His face beamed with interest. "Oh, I hope I get the prize!"

Unexpectedly someone slapped his back—hard! He looked up. It was Tom, leering down at him. "Don't get so excited. If there's a prize, you know who'll win it—and it won't be you!"

"Don will win!" Sandra exclaimed vehemently. "He can draw better than anybody in the room, and you know it!"

Tom sneered. "Don't make me laugh so early in the morning. He hasn't got a chance as long as I'm here. Anything he can do I can do better."

Don started to reply when Miss Caskey walked to the front of the room. "I have a pleasant surprise for you," she told the class. "A drawing contest! We've never had anything like it before. There will be two prizes, a model airplane kit and a paint set."

Exclamations of joy echoed through the room. Tom, sitting a couple of seats away on Don's right, turned and smirked.

It was then that Don remembered the firecrackers. He slipped the package out of his desk along with a few matches. Working under the desk, he carefully removed the soft red paper cover, keeping his eyes on Miss Caskey, who was giving final instructions about the contest.

The sharp, almost spicy odor of powder and fuse came to him as he freed a firecracker from the package. *I'll toss one Tom's way the moment Miss Caskey turns her back*, he thought.

As his teacher turned to the blackboard, Don glanced

down. He had only a few seconds to work. He struck a match. The firecracker was on its way—it was under Tom's desk!

Bang!

The noise was terrific in the closed room. Tom leaped up, waving arms and legs, screaming. In his excitement, Don forgot the burning match in his hand under the desk. Its flame connected with the rest of the firecrackers in the package. An instant later bursting powder sent paper and smoke everywhere.

The room was in an uproar. Students hopped about like popping corn, trying to dodge the miniature missiles. Several firecrackers flew into the air like shooting stars, bursting overhead.

Don ran down the aisle to retrieve the burning pack. He grabbed it. But it burned his hand, and he flung it upward.

Sparkling with fire, it went into orbit near the ceiling, with firecrackers exploding everywhere. The students ducked under the desks. Screams and laughter filled the air.

Then an awful quiet followed.

Don, standing in the center of the room, looked about. The students were disheveled and excited. But not Miss Caskey. She was standing before him with a tight, grim expression on her lips. Her face was pale. "I'm waiting," she said solemnly, "for an explanation."

"It—it was an accident," Don confessed. "I shouldn't have brought firecrackers to school. I'm sorry." He meant to say more, to explain fully, but he moaned instead. His hand hurt as if it were on fire.

Miss Caskey looked at his blistered fingers. "Go to the

principal's office," she said, "and have something put on that burn at once."

He turned to obey, and she placed a hand on his shoulder. "See that this never happens again."

The room and students were in order when Don returned. He sat down quietly and watched the others finish their drawings.

Tom did not win the prize. Neither did Don. In fact, he knew it would be several days before he could even use a pencil.

Looking at his bandaged fingers, he thought, *It wasn't worth it. From now on I won't use firecrackers to cure a show-off like Tom. Or was I the show-off?*

It was a new idea, and he thought about it quite a while. Finally a twinkle came into his eyes. *Well, maybe I was. But this is the last time.* It was a promise he meant to keep.

4

Don't Go Near the Monkey!

by Josephine Cunnington Edwards

t was a pity. It was a shame. There was this one thing about Charlie that was really terrible.

But first let's talk about his good points. He saw something funny in just about everything that happened. True, his contagious good humor got to be a bit distressing to his teachers, for Charlie would laugh out loud about something in the middle of class. Soon the whole room would be laughing before they really saw the joke. Then when Charlie would explain to the teacher, she would get to laughing, too, even before he was through explaining.

Charlie was also a willing helper. If there was work to be done, he would fly at it like he was fixing to kill a bunch of crocodiles.

Charlie had ambition too. When he helped do the dishes, he might not stop till he had cleaned out the oven or put new paper on some of the cupboard shelves. He surprised his mother often by doing things like that. Sometimes she would come home and see him mowing the lawn or sweeping off the front porch.

When he was thoughtful and kind like that, no one guessed that Charlie had a bad habit. It was this: He would decide to do a thing, and once he had made up his mind, no one could change him. A hard look would come into his brown eyes, and he would put his teeth together tight like he was about to bite on a weed or a blade of sour grass.

His whole sweet face would undergo a transformation when that stubborn feeling got inside of him. It would be as if he were saying down in his heart, *I don't care. I am going to do what I want to do, no matter what anyone says. Even if I know I will get a whipping, I am still going to do it.*

Now, that was bad business. But it was there, and Mother studied and worked and prayed about it, and so did Dad and Grandma.

It was especially bad because Dad was pastor of a church, and several of the church members saw Charlie exhibiting that streak of stubbornness. Once in a while someone would say, "Oh, yes, a *preacher's* son."

One day Charlie and Mother went to see Mrs. Jones, one of the church members. She was a particularly talkative woman, and of course Mother wanted Charlie to be good around her, just as she wanted him to be good around everyone. Charlie's pet dog, Brownie, went with them on the visit.

It was a lovely day in summer. The roses were in bloom, and the whole world smelled heavenly with flowers and fresh sweet breezes.

As Charlie and Mother turned up the walk to the house, Charlie saw something very interesting. In fact, he saw two extremely interesting things. He saw a cherry tree loaded with fruit, ripe and red. And under the tree, on a long chain, was a huge monkey.

Charlie had never seen a monkey on a chain before, and he became excited. He loved to watch the monkeys at the zoo going through their funny antics; he could spend a whole afternoon doing that. Now here was a monkey at close range, and under a lovely cherry tree. He stopped, entranced.

"Don't touch the cherries," Mother said, "and don't go near the monkey." She went up to the porch. "The cherries belong to Mrs. Jones, not to you, Charlie, so don't touch them. If she gives you some, all right."

Just as Mother was knocking, she turned again. "Now, *don't* go near that monkey," she repeated. "It looks mean and vicious." She went into the house then and left Charlie with Brownie.

Mother did not look at Charlie as she went in. If she had, she would have seen that ugly look come on his face. His mother hoped he had gained the victory over it; it had been so long since Charlie had looked like that. In fact, for several weeks he had been extra good. He had sorted the potatoes out of the bin, raked the leaves out of the flower bed, and rearranged the bookcase without anyone telling him to. Because he had been so good, Mother had decided to get him a travel book he had wanted for a long time.

Charlie saw Mother go into the house and close the door. He knew he would have several minutes to himself. Maybe even a half hour or longer. Mrs. Jones always talked so much.

He looked at the cherries. Two were lying on the grass. *Mrs. Jones doesn't need those two cherries,* he told himself. *They'll get worms in them if they lie there till tomorrow. And that monkey won't hurt me if I give the two cherries to it. Even wild* animals won't hurt you if you're kind to them. I've read stories about that. I'm not a little baby. I'm ten years old. I can take care of myself.

Charlie reached down and picked up the cherries, which were joined together by their stems. Then he knelt down and held out his hand toward the monkey. It sat beside the tree sullenly watching him.

"Come, monkey, come," Charlie said softly. "Come, I have some pretty cherries for you." He extended his small hand farther, with the fat cherries lying on his palm.

Dimly, he heard his dog whine beside him. Brownie had more sense than Charlie did at that moment. Brownie understood, it seemed, more of what Mother had said.

The big monkey turned its ugly red eyes on Charlie kneeling there, so eagerly extending his hand with the ripe cherries on it. The monkey must have thought the boy was silly, for it had a whole tree full of cherries to eat if it wanted them.

Slowly the creature crept toward Charlie. Charlie thought, *There, now, that monkey is coming right to me. It won't hurt me. It sees I am nice and kind, and it will take these cherries right out of my hand. Then maybe it will let me stroke its head or pet it a little. I can tell the kids tomorrow that I fed a monkey right out of my hand.*

Brownie whined and cried as the monkey drew nearer. Charlie could have seen its yellow teeth and its long sharp fingernails if he had looked. The monkey's eyes were on Charlie, not the cherries. Brownie whined again.

Suddenly, like a streak, the creature lunged. It grabbed both of Charlie's arms with its fingers and closed around them like the teeth of a steel trap. The boy fell backward with a scream, and every long curved fingernail dug a groove of flesh out of his arms. Charlie tried to crawl away, but the monkey seized his leg and sank its teeth into it, up near the knee.

It all happened in a split second. Then a brown streak of fury raced for the monkey. It got the creature by the leg with such a sharp bite that the monkey let go of Charlie immediately and leaped for the top of the cherry tree.

There was so much noise of barking, crying, and monkey chattering that Mrs. Jones and Mother ran out to see what was the matter. There lay Charlie with blood all over his arms and leg. Brownie barked furiously, trying to jump high enough to get at the monkey.

"Your little boy should not have gone near that monkey," Mrs. Jones said.

"I told him not to," Mother replied.

Charlie was so scared and shocked that Mother had to carry him home, big ten-year-old boy that he was. He trembled and sobbed all the way.

That was one time when Mother did not punish Charlie for disobedience—or even scold him. She didn't need to. He knew that every bit of it was his own fault and that no one was to blame but himself.

The scars took a long time to heal. But before they were well, something happened in Charlie's heart that was worth it all. He had a baptism of the Holy Spirit so that he decided to get rid of that stubborn streak in his character. And he really got rid of it forever.

5

Bonnie's Bubble Gum

by Bonnie Moyers

If anyone had asked Bonnie Harver what she thought of Mr. Dobson, her new teacher, she would have quickly replied, "He's the greatest."

Everyone else in the room would have agreed with her. In the first place, they had all been pleasantly surprised when they met him. Instead of being a stern, elderly, gray-haired man, he was twenty-one, handsome, and fresh from college.

He had a pleasant disposition and enjoyed a good laugh as much as the students. His first icebreaking gesture was to ask, "How many of you like to chew gum?"

Hands went up all over the room.

"So do I," he replied. "And since I like to chew it, I'll have to be fair and let you chew it, too, if you like."

"Oh, yeah!" everyone chorused.

"I will, however, make one stipulation," he continued. "Ordinary gum is fine. But there must be no bubble gum. There are few things that can be more distracting when we're having class than to hear *pop, pop, pop* in the background. Am I understood?"

"Yes," the students agreed.

The next day everyone brought gum to school. Mr. Dobson was kept quite busy. As principal, he taught grades seven through ten in the two-room Scranton church school. But he was efficient and well-organized, and things went smoothly in his classroom.

One reason the students obeyed him was that he was impartial. He had no teacher's pets. He loved them all.

The fact that some of his charges were mischievous did not upset him greatly. He remembered that he had been a boy once. He didn't get angry even if an occasional prank was played on him. He took it in stride. If the trick was really amusing, he laughed along with everyone else.

Bonnie was among his more mischievous students. Most of the time she was like a pebble tossed into a quiet pool, her dark-brown eyes merely hinting at the thoughts that lurked behind them. She liked to be where the action was. Whenever anything was going on, she was usually in the middle of it.

She wasn't (and Mr. Dobson would have told you so) a really bad person. Sometimes she even did some nice things. But she had a way of stretching some of the school rules. For instance, she stretched permission to chew gum so that it included a number of other things as well. She frequently sucked chocolate kisses, munched peanuts, or sneaked bites from an apple whenever she thought Mr. Dobson wasn't watching.

She was so clever that nearly a whole semester went by without her getting caught even once. Some of her classmates knew, but they liked Bonnie and didn't want to make trouble by squealing on her.

At the school Christmas party, a bubble-blowing contest was held. Bonnie entered. She could blow bubbles bigger than her head. Her friends watched in fascination as she blew one bubble so huge that it won the contest. The first prize was, not too surprisingly, twelve packs of bubble gum. She made that gum last, chewing only one plug every other day.

But one day Phil, the seventh-grade boy who sat across the aisle from her, leaned over and whispered, "Hey, Bonnie, teach isn't looking. Why don't you blow a bubble?"

Bonnie shook her head. She had never disregarded school rules that openly before.

Phil persisted. "C'mon, he'll never know. Blow a big one."

Again Bonnie said, "No."

But then Phil taunted, "I know why you won't do it; you've lost your touch. You've gone so long without blowing any bubbles that you've forgotten how to."

That was too much for her. She wiggled the gum around in her mouth and started blowing.

Larger and larger the bubble grew. She was planning, when she finished blowing, to suck her breath in gradually so the bubble wouldn't pop when it deflated.

But Phil had other ideas. He stuck the point of his compass into the bubble. *Splat!* It burst, spreading gum all over Bonnie's face.

Mr. Dobson sat, just staring at her for a moment.

A sudden wave of remorse swept over her. "I—I'm sorry," she apologized. "I didn't mean to make a noise."

"I'll let the matter drop this time," Mr. Dobson said. He

was trying hard not to laugh, for Bonnie's gum-splattered face looked so funny! "It seems to me that just getting that sticky mess off your face should be punishment enough," he managed to continue. "But don't let me catch you with bubble gum during class again."

By the time Bonnie looked presentable, she was ready to agree that cleaning the gum off was no picnic. It had stuck to her eyebrows and eyelashes. It was even in her hair. Pat and Ellie had had to help her remove it all.

For several weeks after that she shied away from bubble gum. But the experience had not cured her.

One spring day she decided that a piece of bubble gum would be the perfect way to stretch her lunch period. She wouldn't pop it, of course, or blow any bubbles. She'd just keep it in her mouth and give it an occasional chew. Little did she realize all the trouble that one little piece of gum was going to get her into.

All afternoon it lay hidden in her mouth. No one knew she had it.

Everything went smoothly until ten minutes before dismissal time. Bonnie had played ball at lunchtime without wearing the sweater her mother had insisted she take to school with her. The warm, pleasant morning air had turned cooler that afternoon. Bonnie didn't know it, but she was coming down with the sniffles. Before she could cover her face with her handkerchief, *aaaaaahhh choooh!*

She looked down and saw, to her dismay, that the gum had flown out of her mouth and onto her world history book. She picked the gum up. Should she pop it back into her mouth or throw it away? She didn't get a chance to decide, for Mr. Dobson was looking straight at her. There was no point in attempting to deny her guilt. She had been caught red-handed.

"Bonnie!" Mr. Dobson spoke with as much sternness as his usually congenial voice could muster. "You did it again. One of these days I am going to bring some bubble gum to school and make you chew it all day long."

"Oh, boy," tittered Pat, "that would be fun."

"Would it?" The sternness melted from Mr. Dobson's face and was replaced with a wry half smile. "You'll soon see how much fun it can be."

Pat, Ellie, and Bonnie exchanged anxious glances.

"Oh, well," Bonnie said to them after school, "I'm not going to let what he said worry me. Since he is rather absentminded, he'll probably forget his threat, and we'll be off the hook."

The next day Mr. Dobson did forget. Nor did he remember the next two days. But on Friday morning he sat at his desk with a brown paper sack in front of him.

"Bonnie, Pat, and Ellie," he said as soon as school had begun, "I have a little treat I promised you. Come here."

Reluctantly the three girls walked up to Mr. Dobson's desk. He handed Pat and Ellie each four pieces of bubble gum. "You may sit down now," he said. "Put all the pieces into your mouth. The name of the game is Chew. The rule is that you have to keep the gum in your mouth all day, removing it only for recesses and lunch break."

Next he handed Bonnie five pieces. "Here you are."

"Why did you give me an extra piece?" she asked curiously.

"Because I've caught you with bubble gum more often than I have the others," he explained.

At first having so much gum in their mouths didn't

seem to be such a stiff punishment. But the longer the girls chewed, the bigger the wad seemed to get. Mr. Dobson would not let them get extra drinks to relieve the dryness, which was steadily increasing.

Bonnie felt even more miserable than Pat and Ellie did. Not only did she have a bigger wad of gum, but her sniffles had developed into a full-fledged cold. Her jaws ached. Her throat prickled and burned. She coughed and sniffed.

After a half day with the gum, she decided to ask for a little mercy. "Please," she begged, "let me stop. I have a cold. I feel awful."

"Why didn't you think of those possibilities several days ago?" Mr. Dobson countered. "I won't accept any excuses."

World history class came at one o'clock. The students took turns reading passages aloud from the textbook. When Bonnie's turn came, her mouth was so full she could hardly speak. She read with a definite effort. Everyone laughed when her s's came out as *th*'s.

When her first turn was over and someone else was reading, Bonnie quietly slipped the gum out of her mouth. But Mr. Dobson caught on to that when her turn came to read once more, for she pronounced her words much more plainly.

"Bonnie," he asked, "is the gum still in your mouth?"

"No, sir," she admitted.

"Put it back in, please."

"Yes, sir."

She was close to tears when Mr. Dobson handed her a sixth piece in addition to what she already had. How thankful she was that it was Friday and school let out an hour earlier than usual. She couldn't have stood having to keep that gum in her mouth till three o'clock.

Did Bonnie's punishment cure her of chewing bubble gum in school?

I can assure you it did. In fact, even now, I very rarely chew gum of any kind.

6

A Case of Name Trading

by Dorothy Aitken

t was Mrs. Lawrence's first day as substitute teacher for the eighth grade. As the students began filing into the room shortly after nine o'clock, they noticed the fact at once.

"Hey, a new teacher!" whispered Sharon to Mary Alice. "Let's have some fun with her. She's going to have to be here for at least a couple of weeks, because Miss Adamson is in the hospital. What can we do to liven things up a bit?"

Soon Mrs. Lawrence called the roll. Just before she came to Sharon's name, Sharon turned around in her seat and slipped a note to Mary Alice. The note read: "You answer to my name and I'll answer to yours. She will never know the difference."

When Sharon's name was called, Mary Alice responded meekly, "Here."

A slight titter ran through the classroom, but no one said anything. So the names were all fixed in the very organized and efficient mind of Mrs. Lawrence.

The first day went along very nicely, with the students all grinning behind their books every time Sharon's or Mary Alice's name was called. The next day, however, Mrs. Lawrence chose to give a quiz.

Now, all would have gone well had not Mrs. Lawrence decided to make it a verbal quiz. For Mary Alice was a straight-A student, and Sharon had a hard time staying out of the F bracket. As Mrs. Lawrence gave out the questions, she simply went down the grade book alphabetically and called on the names of the students she wanted to answer.

When she came to Sharon's name, Mary Alice answered the question correctly, and an A went down beside Sharon's name. When Mary Alice saw what was happening, she began to worry. Sure enough, when Mary Alice's name was called, Sharon did not know the answer. Mary Alice groaned when she realized that for the first time in her life she would have an F by her name.

The third day when Mrs. Lawrence was grading the homework, she began to feel that something was not quite right. She noticed that Mary Alice's homework was excellently done; Sharon's was merely half finished, and most of it was wrong at that. She looked back over the grades in the book. Strange, she thought, that in class Mary Alice was getting bad grades while Sharon, who had a long line of failures and incompletes, was suddenly getting A's.

Another day passed with the same puzzling results. By now Mrs. Lawrence's sixth sense told her that something fishy was going on. She decided just to bide her time. She noticed that the two girls seemed to attract a lot of undue attention every time she spoke to either of them. And the sly smiles and winks behind the textbooks did not escape her.

On Friday Sharon was absent. But it was Mary Alice who was marked down as missing in the book. On Monday when Sharon brought her excuse slip, Mrs. Lawrence noted that a lot of erasing had been done on the blank where the name was supposed to be. She looked at it very carefully. The parent's signature at the bottom of the slip had been tampered with.

Closer examination revealed that the original name was much shorter than the one written over it. Then Mrs. Lawrence knew. She pocketed the slip for later reference and went on with class as if nothing had happened.

At recess Sharon heaved a sigh of relief. "I thought for a minute that she had caught on," she whispered to Mary Alice.

"Well, I wish she would," pouted Mary Alice. "You're getting all my good grades, and I'm getting your lousy ones. It isn't fair."

"Don't worry," Sharon comforted her. "Miss Adamson will be back next week. You can stand to give up a few grades for a friend."

Mary Alice wasn't so sure. And when class began the next morning, she was doubly unsure. For Mrs. Lawrence announced an important test. This one, she said, would be oral. It would count heavily on the six-week grade, and anyone who did not make at least a C should not plan on being on the honor roll this time.

Mary Alice sighed. What was she to do? She knew Sharon would fail the test; she always failed tests. But things had gone too far. There was nothing to do but to take the consequences, live through the week somehow, and hope Mrs. Lawrence would never again be assigned to the eighth grade.

When Mary Alice's name was called, Sharon stood up and Mrs. Lawrence put the question to her. "Tell me all you know about the state of Mississippi."

Sharon shifted from one foot to the other. "I—I'm sorry," she stammered. "I don't remember."

"Take your time." Mrs. Lawrence was patience itself.

Mary Alice sat at her desk, her eyes fast filling with tears. Why couldn't Sharon study just once in a while? Mary Alice knew all about Mississippi. She could have recited for five minutes and gotten a good grade.

"I'm afraid I don't know anything about Mississippi," Sharon said weakly, slumping down into her seat.

Others recited, some well, some badly, some not at all. Finally Sharon's name was called. Mary Alive reluctantly rose and came to the front.

"Sharon," Mrs. Lawrence began, looking deep into Mary Alice's eyes, "tell me about the Treaty of Versailles—when it was signed, by whom, where, and what it contained."

Mary Alice began bravely. Almost automatically the words came out.

Mrs. Lawrence watched closely. Soon tears began to roll down Mary Alice's cheeks, and in a moment the girl broke out sobbing. "I'm not Sharon, and it isn't fair that she should get my grades while I have to take her bad ones. Please, I just *have* to make the honor roll. I've never missed being on it since the first grade!" She ran to her seat and put her head in her arms.

Mrs. Lawrence looked at her for a moment. Then she said, "I'm sorry, Mary Alice; you have brought this on yourself. You should have thought about it before you started playing your little joke."

The Great Watermelon Raid

by Dana Kay Merrill

The sun beat down on the heads of the two boys sitting in the back of the old car. Dusting from the dry dirt road curled up behind them.

Mom turned in the front seat. "Jim, did you remember to close the gate to the pasture before we left?"

"Yes, I did," Jim said.

He sighed as he thought of the day the cows got out of the pasture. It *was* kind of funny to see Mom chasing them back in, waving her apron, but now she never let him forget that it was his duty to shut the gate.

The old car steamed to a stop in front of the long, low house of their nearest neighbors, the Jensens. Mom liked to come the ten miles to talk to Mrs. Jensen. So every once in a while Jim and Chuck would pile into the old car, and Mom would drive over to spend the afternoon. The Jensens had no children, so these visits were always a great source of boredom for them.

"You boys play out here on the lawn while I chat with

Mrs. Jensen," Mom said as she turned to go up the long front walk to the house.

The boys sprawled on the grass beneath a tall oak tree.

"Aw, what is there to do anyway?" groaned Chuck. "There's nothing out here but watermelons."

Indeed, there were rows and rows of watermelons growing in the field across the driveway.

"Yup, but wouldn't one of those big, fat melons taste good right about now!" sighed Jim. "It's awful hot out here."

Jim looked at Chuck, and Chuck looked at Jim.

"Are you thinking what I'm thinking?" asked Chuck.

"Let's go!" shouted Jim. Scrambling to his feet, he headed for the patch.

"Now wait for just a minute," called Chuck. "Come back here. This thing has to be planned. You know, the Great Watermelon Raid."

"OK. Get on with it!" said Jim, impatient for the first mouthwatering bite of a juicy melon.

"First, you find out where Mr. Jensen is," Chuck instructed. "We sure don't want to get caught!"

A minute later Jim came panting back. "It's no use. We'll never get those watermelons! Old Jensen is hoeing in the field right next to the patch."

"He won't see us if we keep low," Chuck pointed out. "Those plants are pretty big."

"You mean we're going to crawl the whole length of that field to the other end?"

"Of course not, silly! We'll just pretend we're going for a stroll in those woods at the far end of the patch. Then we'll sneak back and crawl in. It'll be easy!"

"OK, let's go." Jim led the way. "I'm getting hungrier by the minute!"

A half hour later the boys were crawling on their stomachs at the far end of the field. The cool ground in the shade of the vines felt good against their hot bodies.

"Remember, not a sound," whispered Chuck. "Mr. Jensen is hoeing right next to us, you know."

"You just watch out for yourself," returned Jim. "I'm heading for that big, fat striped watermelon right over there."

Inching their way down the rows while rolling five or six giant melons in front of them was no easy chore, but the boys accomplished it. Soon they were sitting in the shade of a tree in the little woods beyond the field.

"Mmm, this is good!" exclaimed Chuck. "Tastes even better than the melons we have at home."

The only answer he received was a happy gurgling sound as Jim buried his face in his melon.

After a while Jim and Chuck sat back to catch their breath.

"Boy, am I ever full," Jim moaned, patting his bulging stomach.

"Do you suppose they'll notice that some of the melons are gone?" asked Chuck.

"Nah, there are hundreds of watermelons out there. They won't miss the few we've taken."

"Boys, oh boys! It's time to go home! Where are you?" That was Mom calling.

"Quick! Get rid of those rinds," said Chuck.

"And wipe your face, too," yelled Jim.

A few minutes later the boys came trotting over to the car, innocent as could be. But after they reached home, Jim's conscience pricked him. Not only his conscience but his stomach felt a little strange too. He had no appetite for supper.

Mom looked at him when he pushed his plate away without emptying it. "Are you sick?" she asked. "I do hope you haven't had too much sun!"

"No, no, I'm fine, really," said Jim, though he had to force the words out. "Excuse me, please." He went up to his room and threw himself across his bed. But his stomach didn't feel any better, and his conscience was still bothering him.

"Hey, are you all right?" Chuck asked, coming into the room.

"No, I feel lousy," Jim muttered. "My stomach hurts horribly."

"Maybe it will go away," Chuck said.

But it didn't, and poor Jim was in misery. Mom put him to bed and called the doctor.

The doctor shook his head and then turned to Mom. "May I see you a moment outside, ma'am?"

Jim, thoroughly frightened now, looked over at Chuck. "Am I going to die?" His voice sounded dreadful.

"Of course not," Chuck said, but he didn't sound as confident as Jim wished he would.

Mom came back into the room, a stern look on her face. "Isn't there something you want to tell me, boys?"

"Yes," Jim said. He felt so sick that no punishment could make him feel any worse; he might as well tell. "I ate some of Mr. Jensen's watermelons today, Mom, and I'm so sorry!"

"So the doctor was right," she responded. "He told me you had probably eaten something that was not quite ripe. I hope you learn a lesson from this. Tomorrow you must go to Mr. Jensen and ask whether there is any way you can pay him."

A week later the boys were hard at work on Mr. Jensen's farm, picking melons and packing them in the back of a truck for shipment into town. Rows and rows of watermelons stretched out before them.

"I never, repeat, *never* want to see another watermelon as long as I live," declared Jim.

"Me neither," Chuck agreed.

8

Scarred Cow!

by Mike Doherty

As soon as morning worship was over, Mr. Lovett, the grounds supervisor, said to Roy and Mike, "I want you boys to take the tractor and trailer and start cleaning the Spanish moss out of the oak trees in front of the school."

After hooking the trailer to the tractor, the two boys drove to the toolshed. There they picked up some equipment and the three freshman members of the grounds crew. As the five boys drove off, Mr. Lovett stepped out of the office and shouted, "Be careful driving that tractor, Roy!"

Mike was sitting on the trailer, and he laughed silently. He knew Roy so well that he was sure Mr. Lovett's words had gone in one of Roy's ears and out the other.

Although Roy often seemed careless, he was a hard worker. And in no time, he and one of the freshmen had cut enough moss off the oak trees to fill the trailer. The next job was to drive to the dump and unload it.

Mike and Roy climbed onto the tractor, and the freshmen scrambled up onto the pile of moss to hold it down.

Roy drove to the dump as though he were going to a fire. Mike, who was used to Roy's antics, watched amused as the freshmen, wild-eyed with terror, groped desperately for something to hold on to.

After unloading, they bolted back to the oak trees for another load. When the trailer was full the second time, it was Mike's turn to drive to the dump. Climbing onto the tractor, he thought smugly, *I'll show Roy and those other guys a thing or two about fast tractor rides.*

Approaching the office on the way to the dump, Mike saw Tom and Mr. Lovett outside.

The boss signaled Mike to stop. "Mike," he said, "I'm going to send Tom along with you this time. Roy, I want you to come with me. I have another job for you."

Mr. Lovett waved the tractor on, and Mike drove slowly until he had gone around the building and through the gate into the pasture. Then he threw the tractor into high gear and jerked back on the throttle. The tractor leaped forward, almost losing its load.

From then on the ride was much the same as the previous ones had been, except Mike took one of the corners so fast that part of the brush slid off and was strewn all over the road. As they came near the dump, Mike saw that the cattle from the adjoining pasture were feasting on the freshly cut moss.

Tom shouted, "Slow down!"

But Mike paid no heed. He continued toward the dump at full speed, proclaiming, "If those crazy cows know what's good for them, they'll move!"

And they did move—all but one of them. The front wheels of the tractor rolled over the cow, pinning the animal to the ground.

The jolt threw Mike under the tractor. But Tom, who had managed to hang on, quickly pressed down on the clutch, stopping the tractor just before the huge rear wheels rolled over both Mike and the cow. After Tom had stopped the engine, Mike shakily crawled out from under it. The other three passengers extracted themselves from the pile of brush that had fallen on top of them.

"Come here and help me get this trailer unhooked and out of the way," Mike called to the freshmen. "Tom, try to back the tractor off the cow."

But Tom's efforts were to no avail.

"Go get Roy to bring the dump truck so we can get the tractor off that cow before it dies," Mike ordered one of the freshmen.

However, just then everyone turned to see the dump truck racing up the road.

Lovett will kill me for this, Mike thought as he watched the truck approach. But as it came closer he breathed a sigh of relief. Roy was driving, with Steve beside him.

Steve, seeing what had happened, jumped out. He pulled a large chain from the toolbox and attached it to the truck and the tractor. Roy backed up, pulling the tractor off the cow.

To everyone's amazement, the cow jumped up and trotted off. It appeared to be in good condition except for a large rectangular burn on its side where the hot oil pan at the bottom of the tractor had touched it.

"Don't anyone go telling Lovett about this. If he ever finds out, he'll fire me for sure," Mike warned.

So all the boys agreed to never mention the incident.

A week passed before Mr. Lovett discovered the injury to the cow. When he did, Roy gave Mike the news. "I was talking to Lovett yesterday, and he said that cow must have had its skin bitten off by another cow."

"What!"

"Yes. He said that when cows get an overdose of horn-growth retardant, they bite each other, and he thinks that's what happened."

"Then I guess I was lucky this time."

Mr. Lovett continued to watch the cow's wound. It didn't heal as fast as he thought it should, so he called a veterinarian. The vet diagnosed the wound as a burn and gave Mr. Lovett some salve to heal it.

The next morning at worship Mr. Lovett asked, "Do any of you boys know what happened to that cow with the burn?"

All of them but Roy denied knowing that the cow had even been injured. Roy was silent. After that the matter was dropped.

April came. Mike was talking to Ellen in the library when Steve walked up. "Guess what? Our friend Roy ratted to Lovett about the cow."

Mike was stunned. He almost didn't go to work that afternoon, but he finally decided to go and get it over with.

Mr. Lovett wasted no words. "If you had told me when it happened, you wouldn't have lost your job. I expect you to pay the veterinarian's bill, and I hope you don't have any trouble getting a new job." He paused. "You're a good worker, Mike, but I can't let a thing like this go."

Mike soon got another job, and one afternoon Roy dropped by. "Hey, Mike," he laughed, "how many cows have you run over today?" It was a long while before Mike heard the end of that kind of joke.

A year and a half went by. Mike was a senior and

was working as a lab assistant in the academy biology department. One afternoon he heard Mr. Viar, the biology teacher, announce to his class in the next room, "To conclude our study of birds, I am going to have Mike take you birdwatching on the property behind the campus."

Birdwatching was one of Mike's hobbies, so he always enjoyed taking the students on such trips. On the walk that afternoon while the students studied birds, he studied the students, especially one of them, Ron. Ron had very little interest in biology or anything that related to it. But as he thought about it, Mike realized that he had quite a lot in common with Ron. Ron worked for Mr. Lovett, just as he himself had when he was a sophomore. And just a week ago, as he had seen Ron go flying down the road on the tractor, he had thought, *He'll learn someday.*

Now, as the group crossed the pasture, something caught Ron's interest. "Hey, Mike, look at that cow! Wonder what made that mark on its side?"

It had been more than a year and a half since Mike seen the scarred cow. He replied nonchalantly, "It's just a scar."

Ron screwed up his face like a question mark. "But how would a cow get a scar *that* shape?" he demanded. "It's sort of rectangular."

"Well, it's a long story," Mike said. And then he proceeded to tell Ron the story of the scarred cow and the sophomore who had learned a few lessons about carelessness and honesty.

9

Conquered by Kindness

by Bonnie Moyers

Ee-e-e-ow!" yelled Albert as he drew his hand back from the chair in front of him.

"What's the matter?" Mr. Sheffield asked. Judging by the expression on his face, he wasn't overly pleased about the way his sixth-grade arithmetic class had just been interrupted.

"Mickey pushed a pin in my hand! She did it on purpose."

"Mickey, I'm surprised at you! Why did you stick Albert with a pin?" Mr. Sheffield wanted to know.

"I did it because he won't keep his hands to himself!" was Mickey's indignant reply. "Every day he thinks up some new way to pester me. Yesterday it was pulling my hair whenever he thought he could do it without your seeing him. Today he has been sticking me with straight pins. I'm sick and tired of it all—so I gave him a dose of his own medicine. Funny, isn't it, how he can dish it out—but can't take it!"

Mr. Sheffield sighed deeply. Of all his problems, the ill

feeling between Mickey and Albert was one of the worst. He knew that their dislike for each other went several years back. Their first spat had occurred in second grade. Albert had pulled Mickey's hair. Mickey had paid him back by rapping him smartly on the knuckles with her wooden ruler. And the feuding had been going strong ever since.

Each one was always trying to get even for the latest misdeed that had been perpetrated upon them by the other. It seemed that they would always be at each other's throat.

Other teachers had thrown in the towel, deciding that there was no way of resolving the problem. Since it apparently could not be eliminated, they tried minimizing it. When Mickey requested that Albert be moved elsewhere so he wouldn't be sitting directly behind or in front of her, they had complied.

All complied, that is, except Mr. Sheffield. He was sure that bringing them together would somehow improve relations between them. So it was that Mickey found Albert seated behind her once more.

"Of all the people you could have put behind me, you chose him!" Mickey's disgust was obvious. "Why?"

"Because," Mr. Sheffield quietly replied, "being in close contact with someone and working with them is the best way to learn how to get along with them. If the two of you would get off each other's back, you might find out that you don't despise each other as much as you think you do!"

But neither of the two students was willing to let bygones be bygones. When they weren't actually fighting, they were fencing verbally. Albert was very good at thinking up insulting names to call Mickey. And Mickey did equally well at giving it back.

After the pin incident, Mr. Sheffield had a talk with Albert and Mickey about Christian kindness and love. "You simply must try to get along better," he urged. "You are sixth-graders, and both of you Christians, yet you quarrel more than some heathens who have never heard of the name of Christ. If you can't get along well together here on earth, how could you ever manage in heaven?"

"Oh, that'll be different!" Mickey smiled wryly. "Heaven will be such a big place that there will be plenty of room for both of us. That way we won't be running into each other very often!"

"I rather doubt that." Mr. Sheffield grinned in spite of himself. "But I'm going to send you into the hall. I want the two of you to sit on the steps facing each other. And I want you to think over what we just talked about. When you think you can come back in and act like decent, civilized people, you have my permission to do so."

As they sat on the steps, looking at each other, Albert remarked, "You know, I feel real silly sitting here like this, don't you? Why don't we call a truce?"

"Good idea," Mickey agreed. "I feel sort of silly myself. I can get along with you if you can with me." So together they reentered the schoolroom.

For a while, Mr. Sheffield's talk and the moments of contemplation spent in the school corridor had some effect. For several weeks Albert and Mickey were almost pleasant to each other. And Mr. Sheffield was secretly congratulating himself that his idea had really worked.

But one day the old trouble flared up again. Albert and Mickey were playing on opposite sides in a horseshoe match. Suddenly Albert howled, "Teacher, teacher! Mickey hit me with one of the horseshoes!"

"Why, Mickey!" Mr. Sheffield remonstrated. "You could hurt someone badly that way!"

"But I didn't hit him—not really. I threw the horseshoe at him, and it whacked him on his shoulder."

"But why did you throw it in the first place?"

"He got mad because I threw a double ringer. So he came up behind me and spit on the back of my neck!"

"I did not!" Albert denied vehemently, his face turning a deep red.

"You did too! I have wet spots on my dress collar to prove it!" Mickey retorted.

"Come here, both of you! Mickey you will stay in for the remainder of lunch period and the two o'clock recess. And Albert, since you started the whole thing, you will stay in during recesses for the next three days. That should give you plenty of time in which to think about mending your ways."

Gloom thickly spread over both Albert's and Mickey's faces. Albert resented Mickey's proving her accusation that he had spit on her. And Mickey found little comfort in the fact that Albert had to stay in longer than she did.

Things simmered down for a few days. Then came another crisis.

Everyone in the upper grades was playing prisoner's base. Albert was caught, and he was determined that Mickey should be too. But Mickey had a few tricks of her own that she used to avoid such situations. She was expert at dodging and zigzagging. Just when Albert thought he had her, she would dodge, then dart off in another direction.

In his effort to keep his eyes on her and follow where she was going, Albert didn't pay enough attention to what was right in front of him. That's why he plowed face-first into a locust tree that grew at the left corner of the playground.

Mickey turned and looked back just in time to see him crash into the tree. She laughed until the tears came.

"All right, what's so funny?" Albert asked angrily, doubling his fists as he spoke. He thought for one fleeting instant that he would like to punch Mickey in the nose so she would know what it was like to hurt as he did. But he rammed his hands into his pockets instead.

"What's so funny?" Mickey was wiping away the tears that her laughter had brought. "You! That's what. You couldn't have done anything crazier if you had been taking idiot lessons! I didn't know you found me so attractive you couldn't keep your eyes off me long enough to watch where you were going!"

"How can you be so heartless and cruel?" Albert asked.

As he turned, Mickey stared at him in amazement. She stifled the remarks she was about to make about people with heads so hard that even bumping into trees wouldn't hurt them, and about her wondering if the tree had sustained any injuries. For Albert really was hurt. He had a large bump on his forehead. It was swelling rapidly. Not only that, but he had a cut that was bleeding profusely. And the whole length of his nose had been scraped. *Why, it must feel like a burn!* Mickey thought, and she knew how bad that could feel.

"Take him in and give him first aid," Mr. Sheffield told Mickey. "That is your department—you're in charge of the first-aid supplies."

Mickey very gently bathed the bump in cold water. Then she applied a styptic pencil to the cut just below it to stop the bleeding. With a swab she put on some antiseptic, then covered the wound with a Band-Aid. She rubbed an ointment on the skinned area, taking most of the sting away.

"There now, does that feel better?" she asked. Strange, but now she didn't despise him anymore. She only felt sorry for him.

"Yes, much better." Albert managed a smile. "You know," he commented, "you'd make a great doctor."

"Thanks!" Mickey flushed at the unexpected compliment. "Oh, and by the way, I'm sorry I laughed at you. I didn't realize at the time how badly hurt you were."

"That's all right," Albert replied. "I have a few things to be sorry for too. I haven't always been so nice to you either."

After that day Mickey and Albert got along fine, and they remained friends all through academy too.

How glad Mickey was that she took that first step and said, "I'm sorry." For though those two words were hard to say, things went so much easier once she had said them!

10

The Perfect Crime

by Penny Estes Wheeler

Beth took a final look in the dormitory room mirror, giving her long black hair a last-minute pat. "You ready to go?" she asked.

"In a minute," Ginger replied. "Let me get a sweater. February is cool, you know, even in Texas, and we've got to walk a mile down the highway."

Beth turned to her redheaded sister. "We have to do it this way," she said. "Otherwise someone might see us getting into Dad's car." She picked up her suede shoulder bag. "Come on, it's getting late."

The girls hurried out their door and down the hall.

"Wait!" Ginger cried as they came to the steps. "We forgot our books."

The two ran back to their room. Beth took out her notebook and history book, opening them on her desk. She threw a pen beside them. Ginger grabbed a library book and opened it, laying it facedown on her bed. As a final gesture she put her hairbrush on the dresser.

Quickly they surveyed their room. Beth pulled out her desk chair slightly and put a magazine on the rocking chair.

"Now," she sighed, "we're ready."

The sisters hurried down the hall and steps. Slowing their pace as they reached the lobby, they walked separately past the desk monitor, past the sign-out sheet, and out the door. In three minutes they were off campus and strolling down the tree-lined road to the highway.

"Whew." Ginger let out her breath in a long sigh. "I feel like I've done a day's work already. This life of intrigue is exhausting."

"You said it," Beth agreed, nodding her head vigorously. "But we had to do it this way. You know good and well that Miss Henderson wouldn't let us go home again—not even for the day. We've already had more than our quota of weekend leaves this semester."

"It's so ridiculous," Ginger fumed. "You'd think we were in some sort of detention home instead of academy, the way they treat us. And we do want to go home today to see Grandma off."

"This way, instead of worrying Miss Henderson about our unnecessary trip—" Beth began.

"She'll be spared an extra ulcer," Ginger finished.

The two doubled over, laughing.

"That was sheer genius to leave our books on our desks as if we were studying," Beth said, still laughing.

"Yeah. No one's going to call us today, but if by some remote chance they do—"

"Our door's unlocked, our books are out, and it looks like we're around somewhere," Beth concluded triumphantly.

"You're sure Jim won't be back until tonight?" Ginger questioned, suddenly serious.

"Positive. When he left on Friday, he said he'd see me Monday. He won't be back 'til after worship because of the bus schedule."

"Well, that's good. It would be something to have him at the dorm asking for you." Ginger paused, thinking. "Let's see. This isn't my Sunday to work, but if someone from the office should call me—oh, well, they won't. There's nothing so important that it wouldn't wait until tomorrow."

The girls stopped under a large pecan tree.

"Dad better get here pretty soon," Beth said. "We don't need to stand here in broad daylight for some faculty member to see." She stepped forward to look down the highway. "Here he comes now," she announced.

Their father stopped the car and leaned across to open the front door. "Hi, kids," he greeted them. "You didn't have to walk all the way to the highway."

"We need the exercise." Ginger laughed. "We didn't mind. Now let's make tracks for home."

"It's nice your dean let you come see Grandma off," Dad said, turning the car toward home. "Grandma will appreciate it. She always misses you girls when she goes to Michigan. Of course, she likes to spend some time with Aunt Jenny and the boys."

"You know we wouldn't let her go without telling her goodbye," Beth said. "Besides, it's exciting going to the airport and watching the planes land and take off."

"There was no problem," Ginger added. "We do need to be back by worship though."

"Plenty of time for that," Dad said. "You girls remember to sign out?"

Beth looked at Ginger and Ginger looked at Beth. Their eyes carried a single message, and Ginger lamely said,

"I guess we forgot to. But no matter. No one will be calling for us."

Grandma appreciated having Beth and Ginger there to see her off. The girls and their parents stayed until they spotted the silver bird fly away.

"We'll wait at home until Grandma calls from the airport in Michigan," Mother said as they got back into the car. "Then we'll take you back to school. You'll be there by six o'clock."

"Fine," Beth murmured. "Plenty of time before worship."

They could hear the telephone ringing as they walked up the steps to their house.

Opening the door, Dad ran inside to answer it. "Beth, it's for you," he said, holding the receiver toward her. "Long distance."

Puzzled, Beth took the telephone. "Hello?" she said, a question in her voice, and a moment later, "Jim! Where are you?"

"I'm at Glenfield, about thirty miles from school," her boyfriend answered. "Where have *you* been? I've been hunting all over for you."

"Oh, no!"

"They paged you in the dorm and you didn't answer, so I called the library, the cafeteria, and even the store. Then I called the registrar's office to see if Ginger was at work, and she wasn't, so I had the operator connect me with the dorm again. The dean went and looked in your room and said you must be on campus because your door was open and your books were open on your desk. Besides, you weren't signed out." He paused for breath. "You still there?"

"I'm still here."

"So I went through the library-cafeteria-store routine again and then decided to ask the dorm for your home telephone number, and this is the second time I've called you here."

"I'm here," she said again.

"Hey, what's the matter? I thought you'd be glad I'll be getting back early," Jim said angrily. "I just have a long layover before I can get a bus."

"Jim," Beth sighed, shaking her head numbly at the telephone, "do you realize that you've just shattered our worst attempts at the perfect crime?"

"Our first and our last!" added Ginger as she looked into the questioning faces of their parents.

11

Don't Bother the Bears

by Todd Lee

"Don't bother the bears," Dad had said again and again. "Bears are bad medicine for boys. You can never predict what they will do!"

"Sure, Dad. Who wants to fool around with a *bear*? If they leave me alone, I'm not going to bother them!" That's what I told my dad, but in truth I wasn't really worried. I guess fourteen-year-old boys just aren't afraid of bears—well, not in the daylight anyway!

Moving from a small town in California to a ranch far out in the wilderness of British Columbia was a tremendously exciting experience for my brother and me. It was a completely new life. Adventure waited at every turn. Our ranch was one of the farthest out from civilization, and beyond its eastern boundaries the forest stretched almost without limits.

At first it was a mystery to us, and we were afraid to venture far from home without Dad along. We didn't know what might be lurking beneath those shadowy boughs.

The stories that neighbors told of bears and wolves and mountain lions were enough to keep us close to the beaten paths. The ranch with its corrals and buildings seemed a snug haven.

As time went by, however, we became bolder. We came to know just what animals lived in the woods. We also learned that stories about their attacking people were only stories, with little or no foundation in fact.

Gradually we discovered that for the most part the animals were more frightened of us than we were of them. So the time came when we roamed the range without fear both on foot and on horseback.

There really were bears in the woods. Occasionally we surprised them in blueberry patches where warm summer days provided them with a feast of fruit. At first we would hastily run in the opposite direction and would tell tall tales at home of the *huge* bear we had seen.

One large black bear stood up on its hind legs, manlike, to peer at us from round beady eyes before it lumbered away. We laughed at its rolling gait, which appeared awkward but was in fact very sure and swift. Certainly the bears could get through the bush faster than we could, and this discouraged any thoughts we might have of trying to keep up with them.

We remembered Dad's warning about bears and other animals, but we couldn't see how these timid creatures could be a danger to us. I guess that's why I became involved in the most foolish and frightening adventure of my life.

The camera I received one Christmas was partly to blame. I was determined to get close-up pictures of as many of our animal friends as possible. It was perhaps too lofty an ambition. But I was encouraged by a bit of luck that gave me a picture of the biggest forest citizen, a bull moose. Intent on cropping the tender buds from a willow, he did not see me approach until I snapped the picture. Then I fled back the way I had come, while he went the other way just as rapidly. I wondered what thoughts he had about this strange two-legged intruder!

But could I get a picture of a bear? That was a real challenge. My brother laughed when I suggested that this would be my next project. And Dad repeated his warning about not bothering the bears.

Well, I would show them. I was determined to fill the page in my album that I had reserved for a bear. Already I had lettered under the blank square some information I had read from a nature book.

One afternoon I rode my pony several miles away to try to get a picture of a hawk's nest that Dad had discovered. I didn't find the nest, perhaps because I had not listened carefully to his directions. On the way home, however, I found another open door to adventure.

I rode into a small meadow and spotted what I at first thought was a black cow mired in the mud of a swampy area. Riding closer, I saw that it was much more. There was, in fact, a cow there, but it was a dead one. Probably it had been killed after it was stuck in the mud, or perhaps it died of natural causes. At any rate it was there, and feeding on it were a large mother bear and two half-grown cubs!

Could I get a picture? Heart thumping with excitement, I studied the situation. The bears had not seen me, but they were too far away to show up in a snapshot. It was then that a possible solution came to my mind. Perhaps I could do two things: discourage the bears from fooling with our cattle and get a picture at the same time.

I determined to see if they would climb a tree. I knew better. I knew that I should have turned my horse and headed in the other direction. That's what Dad would have advised me to do. "Especially stay clear of a bear that has cubs!" he had warned.

For a while longer I waited, daring myself to carry out the plan, half fearful of following my own dare. I guess it was my dog, Duke, that made up my mind. He spotted the bear family and started after them, barking furiously but not going so fast that he would catch up to them. Mother bear took one startled look and turned away, shooing her cubs along with her as they ran for the forest.

I hesitated for only a moment, then gave in to the call of adventure. Could I get the mother bear to climb a tree with her family? Whooping at the top of my lungs, I gave my horse, Dickie, rein and went pounding along the trail in pursuit.

Could Dickie run faster than the bears? Would the bears climb when they reached the woods? I had no idea, but I was going to find out!

That I might run into danger did not cross my mind. Leaning low in the saddle, I urged Dickie forward as fast as he could go, still whooping in chorus with Duke's barking.

As the lumbering trio reached the shelter of the woods, one frightened cub dashed to a large fir tree. It shot up the trunk, its claws tearing chunks from the rough bark. The other cub followed, and both climbed to the first limb. Mother bear whirled and bristled at Duke, her mouth open and teeth bared. Duke skidded to a stop.

"Hi! Hi! Hi!" I shouted.

"*Bow, wow, wow!*" barked Duke.

"*Woof, woof, woof!*" huffed the bear, apparently not at all alarmed now that her cubs were up the tree. She made a threatening move toward Duke, who turned tail and scuttled back to my horse.

Safe above the uproar, the two cubs crouched on their limb and waited to see what would be the outcome of it all.

After making one final feint at Duke, mother bear decided to join her family. With surprising ease she pulled herself up the trunk. Soon all three bears were clustered in branches fifteen or twenty feet above the ground.

"Couldn't be better!" I said, thoroughly pleased with myself.

Now that the ground was free of bears, I felt safe in leaving the saddle. Dickie pranced nervously and snorted her distaste of the whole adventure, and especially of the bears. He was smarter than I.

First I tied Dickie's rein to a sapling. Then I felt free to get on with the job of wildlife photography. Already I was thinking of how surprised everyone would be when they saw the bears' family portrait.

Busy getting my camera ready, I hadn't noticed what was happening in the tree over my head. When I finally glanced up, I was dismayed to see that all three bears were climbing again and had almost disappeared in higher branches.

"Hey!" I exclaimed. "You can't do that! Hold on a minute, will you!"

But the bears continued to climb until all three were clustered in a crotch a good eighty feet from the ground.

Duke looked at me questioningly. What was I going to do next? he seemed to be asking.

"What do you want me to do?" I growled at him. "Climb up after them?"

Duke wagged his tail and looked as though he expected me to do just that!

I was a bit disappointed, but I still had enough sense not to attempt any such thing. Not with mother bear up there ready to protect her cubs.

The idea of climbing had merit, though. Near the bear tree was another large fir that towered even higher. Why couldn't I climb up until I was level with the bears? That way I could remain quite safe and could get a better picture than I had thought possible from the ground.

Climbing trees was something I had been doing ever since I learned to walk. I slung the camera over my shoulder and then attacked the tree, making use of notches in the rough bark for hand and toe holds. When I reached the branches, the climbing got easier. Finally I sat on a large limb almost directly across from the bear family.

What luck! Trembling with excitement, I gripped the limb firmly with my legs and prepared to snap a picture. Oh, no! The shutter was stuck! On closer inspection I discovered that the trip lever had jammed.

Like time, bears wait for no one. I suppose that mother bear was nervous because of my closeness to her cubs and suspicious of my intentions. Before I had freed the lever, I heard a clawing and scraping. Looking across, I saw her furry black coat disappearing down the trunk of her tree. The cubs didn't follow her, but they squirmed around until the tree all but hid them from sight.

What now? While I fumed with impatience and indecision, Duke's wild barking told me that the bear had reached the ground. Was Duke chasing her, or was she chasing Duke? The tone of Duke's bark seemed to indicate that the latter was the case.

Then a horrible thought dawned on me: What if she should climb up my tree?

For a moment I was almost dizzy with terror. I looked down the tree, but I couldn't go down—the bear was there! I looked up to the branches above me, but mother bear could climb as high as I. Across the twenty feet of space I saw the cubs peeking around the tree trunk. They were trembling and whimpering and looking anxiously from me to the confusion going on below.

I thought, *They are just as frightened as I!*

In that moment I felt ashamed for what I had done, terrorizing the bear family just for a picture, forgetting about Dad's warning. How foolish I had been! I gripped the branch until my knuckles turned white while waves of fear swept over me. "Oh, God," I whispered, "forgive me for not obeying Dad. I didn't mean to be so foolish. Don't let that bear climb my tree!"

I guess God must keep special watch over boys, knowing how impetuous and scatterbrained they can be. A few moments later I saw the bear leading Duke off in a vain pursuit into the surrounding timber. Perhaps she had forgotten all about me and was just luring the dog away from the tree in which her cubs waited. Well, if that was what she wanted, I was glad to go along with her idea. I fairly flung myself down the tree, sliding down the lower trunk with a rush and landing in a heap.

Dickie was gone. I suppose that when mother bear and Duke were playing ring-around-the-rosy, he had decided that enough was enough and had snapped the rein that held him to the sapling. I knew he would be waiting for me at the pasture gate at home.

"So long, fellows. Sorry!" I shouted up at the cubs.

Then I took off in the opposite direction from that taken by the bear.

There would be many more adventures in this northern wilderness, but I had learned a valuable lesson about relations with our animal neighbors. Never again would Dad have to warn me not to bother the bears!

12

A Few Laughs

as told to Judy Wright

About 9:30 this past Saturday night after a movie, a few of us guys were just hanging around the academy dorm. Ed was there, and Rick (my roommate), and Dennis, and a couple of his friends. We were in Ed's room, and all of us were pretty bored.

Dennis picked up the *Student Handbook* and started reading from the front where it describes the school. It was pretty funny the way he did it—like he was Elder K, the principal. Dennis is a great mimic.

He adjusted his glasses, cleared his throat, straightened an imaginary tie, and began: "I'm ready if you are, boys."

We stopped talking and gave him our attention.

"There, there, that's *so* much better. This is beautiful Basswood Academy, established in 1914. This picturesque spot offers many opportunities for student growth. Located on Highway 17, seven and one-half miles from the town of Dullsville—"

I must admit Dennis edited a bit here and there.

Anyhow, he had finished reading almost the whole first page—with an occasional pause to clear his throat, push back his glasses, et cetera, and we guys just sat there and let him. Why not? We had nothing else to do. The movie was but a memory, and not that exciting a memory either, because only seniors can date when movies are shown.

"Basswood Academy owns and operates a dairy and a Harris Pine Mills, in addition to the new frozen foods industry added in 1970," Dennis continued. "Here, as well as on the campus, the willing student worker may—"

"Hey!" Ed jumped up. "I've got an idea! I just thought of something."

"Does thinking hurt that bad?" asked Dennis reproachfully.

Ed just glared. "No, really. I know what we can do to brighten up this whole scene." And he described the most delicious scheme. It was a masterpiece.

It had been voted somewhere up there in a higher sphere than student-faculty council that the farm should be enlarged. As a result, late Friday afternoon a shipment of bawling cattle had been deposited in an old corral-type place quite a ways from the barn. I think they were all heifers, but I'm not a farm worker, so I'm not sure. Anyhow, we *were* sure they were there.

So as soon as lights were out and our monitor had done his last rounds for the evening, we snuck out and headed for those cows. We decided to go across the fields rather than by the road. And although battling mud, rocks, and stickers to get under an electric fence isn't much of a blast, it does beat sitting in the dorm reading the *Student Handbook*.

Finally we reached the cows. "They sure have a lot to say," Ed whispered.

"Who volunteers to use this?" Rick held up the rope he had brought along.

Nobody volunteered. I don't know about the other guys, but I'd never even *touched* a cow before, let alone roped one. Finally we went hand over hand the length of the whole rope, like it was a baseball bat, to decide.

Some people are luckier than others. Specifically, five guys were luckier than one guy—me. I won.

"You've got to help me," I insisted.

So we climbed over the last fence. All those spooky, mooing cows just kept staring at us and backed up, their white faces shining in the moonlight. At first we walked slowly and held out our hands and said, "Here, cow, nice cow." But we felt pretty stupid.

All of a sudden Ed yelled, "Hi-ho, Silver—ride 'em, cowboy!" and waved his arms and ran at the cows. Then we took off after them, shouting like idiots.

Oh, it took us a while, but in the end we proved that boys are smarter than cows. We had our cow on the rope and out the gate.

"Be careful," Dennis warned. "The farm manager would be pretty sore if we turned the whole herd loose."

"He'd have a good reason to be—as hard as these beasts are to catch," agreed Ed.

But we had plenty of time to secure the latch behind us, and the remaining cows showed no interest in escaping. They weren't exactly following us around, so we needn't have worried.

Now we had to take the road to the dorm, and we went along with fear and trembling. It must have been near midnight, and kids out of the dorms at that hour have been known to meet the night watchman, Mr. Ferris. And we had one four-legged member of our party who was not cooperating to the extent that she would lie down in the ditch if we saw someone coming.

Dennis started clowning: "Why, hello, Mr. Ferris. Beautiful night, isn't it? Cow? Why, *Mr. Ferris!* How impolite. You know how sensitive Fred is about his size."

So we hurried along the road, and no—we *didn't* meet the night watchman. We made it right to our destination—the flagpole in the center of campus. And we tied the cow there, left her grazing, and returned to the dorm—feeling pretty smug, I might add.

The dean was not waiting for us at the door, or in our rooms. We just went to bed and to sleep, carefully setting our alarms so as not to miss the reactions at breakfast.

The reactions were gratifying. Nothing like a cow tied to the flagpole in the middle of campus to cheer up a person.

All day Sunday was beautiful. Laughter and cheer everywhere we went.

I would like to say "The End" and be done with it now. I'd really like to do that. But there's a bit more to tell.

At the end of the joyous Sunday came evening worship. At the end of evening worship came Elder K. *He* wasn't laughing.

He just said very quietly, "There are several boys I want to see in the dean's office immediately after worship. I don't know your names, but you're the ones responsible for the presence of the cow in the middle of campus this morning."

That was all—but somehow we felt we were in for it.

It was pretty hard to go to that office after worship. Some of the guys didn't want to go at all, but in the end we went. And it wasn't entirely our spotless characters that prompted us. Even if we could quiet our consciences, word was spread pretty liberally all over campus who we were. Somebody's conscience was sure to be bothered over our project, even if ours weren't. Still, it's a good thing Elder K is a patient man, because it took us a while to work up enough nerve.

When we were all in the office, he closed the door and just stood there for a bit. Then he asked, "Have you boys ever heard of shipping fever?"

We all looked blank.

"The cow you tied to the flagpole is dead," he said. "Several others are pretty sick, and we won't know for a while whether they'll pull through or not."

Then we learned that when cows are shipped they get shipping fever, and a lot of excitement right away can make things really bad for them.

Fortunately, only the one cow died—and even though it seems that it will take the six of us until we're on Social Security to work it off in free labor, at least we weren't sent home.

I've always hated those stories about practical jokers who end up in trouble. A few laughs never hurt anyone, I always said. But I don't believe that anymore—and I'm not so sure that practical jokes are all that funny.

13

Flying Machine

by Andrew Demsky

Let's build a hang glider," Roy said.

"Oh, right, like that car you built," Rocky snorted. "Went about three feet and fell apart."

I just shook my head. Roy and Rocky were brothers and good friends of mine. Both were crazy, but Roy was definitely further out in nutland than the rest of us. For weeks now he'd been harping on this idea of building a hang glider.

"Look," Roy went on, "I saw these guys when I was in Tennessee. They had these hang gliders and just took a running jump and sailed right off."

Roy demonstrated this idea with his hands soaring up over his head. "They could stay up there for hours if they wanted to."

"They could get killed too," I pointed out.

"Well, not if you know what you're doing," Roy shot back.

"And where are you gonna jump off around here?" Rocky asked. "The barn?"

Roy looked over at the huge white barn. It rose about fifty or sixty feet high at the peak of its sharp roof. "Maybe later, when I get some practice."

Rocky looked at me and rolled his eyes.

"Maybe the goat shed," I chipped in sarcastically.

Rocky looked over at the shed and laughed too. "There you go, Roy!"

But Roy's coconut-shaped head rose proudly on his skinny neck, letting us know that he was above our tiny minds and our tiny doubts. "You guys don't take me seriously, but I'm gonna build this thing and I'm gonna fly off the goat shed, and you're gonna be sorry you didn't help."

Roy had this way of making whatever he was planning to do sound like a once-in-a-lifetime chance. If you missed the opportunity, it would never happen again.

I noticed that Rocky was laughing uncomfortably. "You'll never even get off the ground."

Roy sucked in his lower lip thoughtfully. "Maybe not. But what if I do? Huh?" His voice picked up speed. "What if the wind picks me up and carries me up over the house and out across the pasture and beyond the train tracks? What then?"

"Won't your mom get mad if you do that?" I asked.

Roy paused. "Well, I'll just turn it around and come back. You can kinda control where you go—you knew that, didn't you?"

"Well, sure."

"Of course it's dangerous . . ." Roy picked up a stone and threw it at the birds sitting on the telephone wire. "Guys get killed all the time on these things. They land and crash and break all their arms and legs. Sometimes they never walk again."

"I told you," Rocky said.

Roy shrugged. "Just a risk you gotta take." He flung another rock. "Gotta be a man."

That did it. Nobody was going to make me into anything less than a man. I counted myself in on the project, with Rocky reluctantly following.

Building a hang glider took longer than we expected. First off, none of us were sure exactly what it should be made of. The only thing we knew for certain was that it should look like a big kite. We'd all made kites before, so it seemed logical that all we had to do was make a kite that was about fifty times larger than normal. Plus we'd have to rig up some way to keep Roy attached to the thing, a handlebar or a sling of some sort.

We managed to nail together a rough frame from scraps of wood. It seemed flimsy, so we tied weight-bearing sections together with twine, then covered the twine with Elmer's Glue.

Roy knew his life would be on the line, so if we were going to do it, we were going to do it right.

With the skeleton finished, we needed a covering. We figured paper would be too weak, so we searched for something tougher. Rocky found some sheet metal, and Roy said that was too heavy. I suggested the tarp that covered the speedboat in the backyard. Roy and Rocky both shook their heads in fear—their father would skin them alive! At last someone found an abandoned sheet of clear plastic, left over from when Roy was going to build a greenhouse.

We laid the plastic sheet over the wooden glider frame, cut away the excess, and nailed it to the frame. By then we'd run out of glue, so the nails alone had to do. Rocky and I voted against a special bar for Roy to hold on to, thinking he could just hang on to the sides of the glider. Roy disagreed. Scrambling through the junk boxes in the garage, he triumphantly produced rusted handlebars from an old bicycle. Rocky and I wearily helped Roy attach the handlebars to the underside of the glider.

At last it was finished, and we hauled the oversized kite outside. The wind was beginning to pick up.

"Perfect glider weather," Roy confided to me.

We helped Roy to the top of the goat shed and handed up the glider. It seemed a little heavy, but Roy was excited. Nothing was going to stop him now. His face was beet red with exhilaration. You could tell that he truly believed that five minutes from now he'd be soaring high above the earth.

The wind whipped through his hair. (He said the wind was much stronger up there on top of the shed. After all, the shed was nearly six feet high.) The goats watched in silent stupidity as Roy lifted the glider above his narrow head. He took two steps; the wind tugged fiercely at the glider.

Suddenly there was a ripping sound and the glider flew up into the air, flipped once, and dropped into the goat pen. Roy was left standing on the shed, holding the handlebars above his head.

Rocky began to laugh.

"It's not funny! Go get it!" Roy commanded. "And hurry up!"

Rocky and I retrieved the glider, now scratched and torn in a couple places. Wrestling with the wind, we handed it back up to Roy.

Now Roy bravely gripped both edges of the glider. The fast wind pulled the nose up, jerking the thing around in his hands.

Rocky laughed and turned away. "This is never going to work," he said privately to me.

The goats had returned and stood watching, waiting.

Roy made his way to the edge of the roof, and suddenly—

"Roy Waldo Wheelwright, you come down off that roof this instant!"

It was the voice of their mother, who was walking up the driveway.

"His middle name is Waldo?" I asked.

"Yeah," Rocky chortled.

Roy froze at the edge of the roof. Suddenly I realized he was teetering! As if in slow motion, Roy and the hang glider tipped over and crashed into a single heap on the ground.

Now the Wheelwright brothers' mother headed for the pile that was Roy and his flying machine. Reaching into that mess of plastic, wood, twine, and Elmer's Glue, she pulled Roy out by one ear, kind of like a magician pulls a rabbit out of a hat. Without a word she dragged him to the house.

The last words I heard from him were "Come over tomorrow—I think I know what we did wrong!"

Rocky looked at me; then we both glanced over at the crumpled-up hang glider. Somehow we knew there would be no tomorrow for Roy and his flying machine.

14

The Truth About Meany Volteeni

by Karl Haffner

Got a joke for you," Paul said to his brother Randy. "What's the best thing to do if you're going to be beheaded by Meany Volteeni?"

Randy was usually good at solving Volteeni riddles, but this one was a stumper. "I don't know; what?"

"Stay calm and try not to lose your head," Paul replied, erupting in laughter.

"I've got one," Randy shot back. "What is Meany Volteeni's favorite plant?"

"What?"

"Poison ivy!"

The joking continued while they worked on their go-cart. Paul adjusted the carburetor while Randy checked the oil. Soon the engine was purring like an Indy race car.

"Hey, there's Vinnie," Paul said, looking up, "the guy who moved into Fiorellos' house. Let's have him take the go-cart for a test spin."

Vinnie was delighted. He squealed out of the driveway

and raced around the block a couple times. When he pulled back into the driveway, he had a smile plastered on his face. "This is awesome! Can I run it again?"

"Maybe tomorrow," Paul said. "We have to park it now because Mr. Volteeni's car is in his driveway."

"So? Who's Mr. Volteeni?"

"He's the old man in the white house at the top of the hill. Every time we ride the go-cart, he calls the police. They should be coming—"

"Yep, and here they are," Randy interrupted, pointing to a police car cruising by.

"We call him Meany Volteeni because he hates kids," Paul explained. "Rumor has it he killed Tony's cat last year."

"Why would he kill a cat?"

"To eat it—or feed it to his pet snake."

"He has a snake?" Vinnie asked in disbelief.

"Well, we don't know for sure," Paul whispered, "but we think so, because his drapes are always closed. He's hiding either a pet or an ugly wife."

"Maybe both!" Randy joked.

The police officer crept by again, glaring suspiciously at the boys. Vinnie shifted nervously. Paul and Randy maintained their composure.

"I don't know why Meany Volteeni is so concerned about the law," Randy said. "He's the one who has a fake handicap tag. Maybe we should report *that* to the police."

"He's not handicapped?" Vinnie asked.

"In the brain maybe, but he walks fine," Randy answered. "He's just too lazy to walk from a regular parking spot."

As the long days of summer dragged into fall, Vinnie heard more horror stories about Meany Volteeni. Except for glimpses of him driving by, however, Vinnie never saw him—until the kickball game.

With the score at five to four in the third inning, Tony belted a shot that soared into Meany Volteeni's front yard. Bursting out of the front door like a tiger on fire, Mr. Volteeni dashed to the ball, scooped it up, and returned inside.

"Hey, he can't do that!" Vinnie cried out.

"He just did," Paul said. "Looks like you lost a ball."

"But what—"

"Forget it, Vinnie," Paul advised. "Meany Volteeni has a new ball."

"But what will he do with a kickball?"

"He'll probably feed it to his snake—or his wife."

The kids scattered in every direction while Vinnie stewed over his lost ball. "He won't get away with this," he muttered. "I'll get even."

In the months that followed, Vinnie schemed how to get even. After he contrived a plan, he enlisted the help of Paul and Randy. "It's perfect," Vinnie gloated. "On Halloween night we'll toilet-paper his house. Then we'll decorate it with eggs, and maybe spray-paint the score of our last kickball game—that is, till he stopped it."

"But what if he calls the police?" Randy protested.

"Of course he'll call them," Vinnie answered. "But the cops won't bother with a toilet-paper call on Halloween night when they have gangs running wild all over town!"

Before Paul and Randy could protest any further, Vinnie unfolded his hand-drawn map of the Volteeni property. "Paul, you'll come up from the woods at this angle. Randy, you and I will sneak under the porch with the supplies and wait for the signal from the street. We'll get Tony to cover that post. When we get the signal, we'll strike quickly. Any questions?"

They shook their heads no. By Halloween night the details of Operation Toilet Paper had been fine-tuned. The boys scurried to their posts and waited for Tony's whistle. At the signal Vinnie dashed to the garage and started unrolling the Charmin.

As Vinnie reached into his knapsack to reload his ammunition, he caught a glimpse of Mr. Volteeni in the kitchen. He stared through the shades, motionless. Shaking the disturbing image from his mind, Vinnie continued with the task at hand.

When they finished throwing eggs at their masterpiece, the boys left in a chorus of giggles and high fives. Glancing back, they admired the white house accented with their "yellowyolka polka dots."

A victory celebration in Paul and Randy's fort followed the ransack. But no matter how hard Vinnie tried, he couldn't enjoy the party because of what he had seen through Mr. Volteeni's window.

The image faded with the frigid Rhode Island winter. It wasn't until his birthday in March that Vinnie's dad jogged his memory. "I finally met that Volteeni guy that you and your friends keep talking about," his dad said as Vinnie started opening his presents.

"Really?" Vinnie asked.

"Yeah, I asked him to sign the petition asking the city not to put a landfill on Maltby Avenue."

"Did he sign it?"

"Sure. He doesn't want his property to depreciate any more than the rest of us. By the way, did you know his wife is in a wheelchair?"

"Yeah," Vinnie said, remembering the Halloween ransack.

"Do your friends know about what happened?" his dad probed.

"No. I think I'm the only one who knows about the wheelchair. But I don't know why. Do you?"

"Yes," his dad answered. "I got to talking to him and asked him."

"And?"

"And what?"

"And how did it happen?" Vinnie insisted.

"He got in a car wreck back in 1974. I guess he'd been drinking, and, well, as he put it: 'Booze cost me my seven-year-old boy and my wife's body—and mind.' "

"Is that why he doesn't like kids—because they remind him of his boy?"

"I don't know, Son. Maybe you should ask him sometime."

Vinnie felt a strange churning in his stomach. For the first time since seeing Mr. Volteeni's wife through the shades, he felt a peculiar sympathy for Mr. Volteeni. Maybe he and his friends had judged the man too harshly.

After Vinnie had created a mess with opened boxes, ripped paper, and gifts, his dad brought out the last present. The smile on his face heightened the suspense.

"Here you go, Vinnie," he said. "We saved the best for last."

"What is it?" Vinnie asked.

"Open it and see," Dad answered as he steadied his camera.

"All *right!*" Vinnie squealed as he ripped into it. "A new kickball. I've been needing one of these."

"Look at it more closely," Dad coaxed.

"Hey!" Vinnie exclaimed as he examined the ball. "This isn't new. This is my old ball! How'd you get this?"

"All I had to do was ask," his father said with a smile.

15

Saved by the Belt

by Melanie Bockmann

Why can't I take it?" Stan asked, agitated. "I'm not a little kid. I'll be careful with it."

Stan's mother shook her head decisively. "No more arguing. The bow-and-arrow set stays here. Accidents can happen, even when you're careful. Besides, there will be so much to do at the church picnic today you won't even miss it. Now, help your dad get the car loaded, please, so we can go."

Stan sulked as he carried food and blankets to the car. He had told his friends all about his new bow and the arrows with real metal tips. And he had promised to show it all to them. Now, because of his overprotective mother, he was going to have to leave them at home.

They're going to think I was bluffing about the whole thing, Stan thought angrily. He made a face and kicked some rocks with the toe of his shoe. "Accidents happen, even when you're careful," he mimicked his mother's words. "How totally stupid!"

Stan went into his room and shut the door. "I can't believe this. I'm fourteen years old, and my parents treat me like I'm seven. Sometimes I wish they would just let me make my own decisions." He picked up an arrow and ran two fingers down the length of it in awe. "Boy, this baby sure could fly!"

"Stanley! Come on. We're ready to go!" Stan's mother called from outside.

"I'm just getting my jacket," Stan called back. He started to leave, then quickly wrapped his new bow and arrows inside his coat and ran outside.

"I'm sorry you couldn't bring your bow and arrows, Son," Stan's mother said as they pulled into the parking lot at the park. "It's not that I don't want you to have a good time; it's just that there will be so many people here it would be easy to hurt someone accidentally."

"It's OK, Mom; I understand." Stan wriggled uncomfortably. "I'll just, uh, wade in the stream with my friends, or something."

He began to feel so guilty that he almost wished he'd left the set at home. *I'll just show it to Tony and Jake and then put it back in the car*, he decided to himself. *Mom and Dad will never even have to know about it.*

Stan made sure that his friends were behind the bushes before he pulled his choice new possession out to show them. They were definitely impressed.

"Wow!" Jake said enviously. "I wish I had one."

"Can I try it?" asked Tony.

"No, you'd better let me handle it," Stan said. "These things can be pretty dangerous."

The more his friends admired the set, the less guilty Stan felt about disobeying. After all, he was being super careful with it. Maybe he'd just try it out once to show them how it worked.

"I say you can't hit that rock across the stream from here," Jake challenged.

"I say I can," Stan bragged. He fit an arrow into the bow, aimed, and stretched the cord back as far as he could until his arm muscles quivered.

Ping! The arrow whizzed through the air and across the stream toward its intended target. The boys cheered. Stan grinned and pushed his hair out of his face. This was so cool!

Then all at once the cheering stopped. The arrow hit the rock and ricocheted off in the direction of the bushes where the picnic tables were located.

"Oh, no!" Stan's heart seemed to stop as the arrow flew past the boys.

Whish! The arrow hit the bushes like a bolt of lightning, stripping the leaves right off the branches. There was a loud thud—and then a long, tormented groan.

"It hit someone!" screamed Jake.

The boys ran around to the other side, and there on the ground was Stan's father, clutching his abdomen and moaning in pain. Everyone gathered around, wondering what to do. Stan knelt down beside his father, terrified. "Dad?"

Dr. Sever, who had also come to the picnic, pushed his way to the center of the group, where Stan's father lay. "Let me take a look, Dan," Dr. Sever said. He pulled up Stan's father's shirt to examine the area. Already there was a bruise the size of his hand on his stomach.

Stan's mother gasped.

"Thank God," Dr. Sever said as he pointed to Stan's

father's belt buckle. "Your guardian angel was looking out for you today, Dan. This saved your life. If it hadn't been for this belt buckle, that arrow would have gone right through you."

Stan shuddered as he stared at the dented belt buckle. His disobedience had almost cost his father's life. "I'm so sorry," Stan said tearfully as he looked at his parents. *I'm sorry to You, too, Lord,* he prayed silently.

Stan reached down, picked up his new bow and arrows, and handed them to his mother. This was one mistake he would not make again.

16

Pool Rules

by Melanie Bockmann

"**E**verybody in the car!" Dad called. "It's sunny, and we're going swimming!"

After my family moved to the Pacific Northwest, we realized quickly that if we slept in on a sunny day, we could easily miss spring and summer altogether. If the sun broke through the clouds, everyone wore sunglasses and shorts— even if it was only thirty degrees outside.

This was one of those rare and celebrated sunny days. The community pool had thawed considerably, so we donned our swimsuits and headed downtown. We probably could have fit the whole town in the pool, and on that particular day, I think we almost did.

"Soak in the vitamin D, kids," Mom advised as we walked through the gate and tested the water with our toes.

I thought about wading into the shallow end first, but it looked like a toddler hatchery. So I decided to follow Dad and my brother to the less-populated deep end with its diving boards.

"Put your toes just over the edge of the board and then dive in," Dad instructed my brother.

"Like this?" my brother asked, then did a belly flop.

Dad grimaced. "Good try."

I climbed up the rungs to the board.

"Keep your body straight!" Dad coached from the ground.

From the edge of the board I noticed the young lifeguard on his chair. He was busy telling stories of how brave he was during his last rescue effort and collecting phone numbers from the impressed female population. The funny thing was, I had witnessed his latest "rescue" effort. His bottle of suntan lotion had fallen into the pool, and he'd used the net to retrieve it.

Good thing nobody's really drowning, I thought.

My diving effort wasn't much better than my brother's, and I could see that Dad's hopes for our being in the Olympics were fading.

"Hey, Dad," my brother called. "Do a cannonball!"

My father climbed up onto the board and laughed. "You asked for it!"

He leaped off the board high into the air and tucked his body into a ball before hitting the water with a splash.

Suddenly there was a piercing whistle blast from the lifeguard. Dad came up from under the water, and the pool went silent.

"You, over there!" the lifeguard called on his megaphone while pointing at Dad. "The sign says 'No Splashing.' Get out of the pool and sit on the bench!"

No one moved. We waited to see what Dad was going to do. Kids stopped splashing, and mothers at the edge of the pool let their sunglasses slide down their noses so they could have a better view of what was about to happen. The girls surrounding the lifeguard chair smiled admiringly at their hero as tension mounted. I stood on the side of the pool, waiting for Dad to give the little punk a piece of his mind.

But he didn't.

Silently he climbed out of the pool, walked over to the bench, and sat down. Gradually the decibel level of the pool climbed back to normal, and the lifeguard went back to sunning his epidermis.

I couldn't believe it! Walking over to the bench, I plopped down next to my dad.

"I don't get it," I said. "You know that guy's about my age, and he's just showing off. You don't have to sit here and take this from him."

Dad took the towel and began drying his face. "Well, I admit that thought crossed my mind. But according to Romans 13:1, I do need to sit here."

"Why? Does it say, 'Thou shalt let a kid on a power trip embarrass you in front of a whole town'?"

Dad laughed. "Well, not exactly. But it does say that everyone must submit to the governing authorities. At this pool the lifeguard is the governing authority."

"But Dad—"

"If I didn't sit here," he interrupted, "I would be telling other people that I don't have respect for authority, and that's wrong. God may not have specifically put Mr. Suntan over there in charge, but He developed the idea of rules and authority so that everything would run smoothly. If everyone thought they were above the law, we'd have chaos."

"I understand that part, but that guy over there is nothing but tan skin wearing sunglasses. He's not even a responsible lifeguard!"

Dad smiled. "Maybe. But it's still my responsibility to respect his authority over the pool. It's his responsibility to deserve that respect. He hasn't done that too well today. But fortunately, I don't have to answer for his actions, just for mine."

Before long the lifeguard signaled that Dad could get up from the bench and return to the pool.

"But no more splashing," I teased as we padded to the water.

"You'd better be careful," Dad teased back. "I'm your governing authority, and I'll make you sit on the bench for the rest of the summer!"

I guess that day Dad was trying to tell me that not every situation is going to be fair, and not every authority figure is going to be worthy of respect; but sometimes it's better to know you're doing the right thing. Even if it means sitting on the bench.

17

Hot Stuff

by Randy Fishell

The Michigan Fire Maniacs was a fun-loving group of five young teens. Together they boasted an IQ that matched the local fire department's opinion of them—very low. I write with some authority on this topic as a former, card-carrying member of this wacky outfit.

The Brawley brothers had invited several of us guys over to their grandparents' farm for Sabbath lunch. After we'd inhaled the last of Grandma Brawley's fine apple pie, the five of us politely excused ourselves and set off in search of some fine Sabbath afternoon mischief.

Quickly Spike Brawley and Buddy Mitchell steered us in the right—er, wrong—direction. Over the driveway and through the field to Grandmother's woods we went.

Understand that summer Michigan woods approach the fire potential of a Kuwaiti oil field in a drought. That's why I questioned the wisdom of Spike's pulling a few fire-crackers and a book of matches from his pocket. *Something tells me this is a very bad choice*, I thought.

"These babies came from Tennessee," Spike informed us. "Got 'em on the way back from our vacation in Florida."

We watched with some admiration as Spike struck a match and put it to the fuse. A split second later a loud *bang!* shot through the woods.

"Hey, Spike, you'd better cool it," his usually quiet brother, Lester, warned. "They might be able to hear the blast at the house."

The thought of his father striking out through the woods in search of his wayward son was enough to derail Spike's fireworks display. Instead, he decided to build a fire.

"Let's see how much smoke we can make out here," he suggested, arranging leaves in a neat pile.

"Bu—but," Lester spoke again, "don't you think they'll see the smoke back at—?"

Too late. With a quick flick of his wrist, Spike set the pile ablaze.

The experiment proved a roaring success. Flaming leaves, caught by the gentle summer breeze, soon spawned several small ground fires in Grandma Brawley's woods. We all leaped into another fine Sabbath afternoon activity— firefighting.

"This one's out!" came a harried cry from the east.

From the west a panicky voice said, "Then get over here!"

From my recollection of those moments, anyone viewing this scene might have mistaken us for a group of deep-woods religious fanatics practicing a secret ritual dance—the Sabbath fire stomp.

Pausing to catch my breath, I glanced up into the trees. *They* were on fire! The situation seemed too hot for us to handle.

"Spike!" I shouted. "You'd better move it to the house and get some help!"

By now Spike sensed that a well-paddled behind would sit better than a stint in the state penitentiary as a full-fledged arsonist. Without looking back, he shot off through the woods to 'fess up and secure assistance.

Speaking of fire . . . I have no idea what happened back at Grandma Brawley's house, but I like to imagine Spike's dad sitting in the living room with an interested non-church-attending dinner guest, talking religion.

"Yes, the book of Revelation says clearly that in the end the wicked will be destroyed by—"

"*Fire!*" Spike screams as he flies into the room, out of breath.

The dinner guest's eyes grow wide. Spike's father's eyes grow narrow. Spike realizes that soon there will be weeping and gnashing of teeth.

Before Spike returned to us, the wail of the volunteer fire department's siren had already filled the air. The woods became filled with flurried activity. Most of it came from the firefighters' eventual victory over the flames. But some of it occurred behind a large tree where Spike and his dad had headed off together for a postfire season of discipline.

All of which leads me to say that it's never too late to start making good choices. Nowadays I spend my Sabbaths doing things that are unlikely to arouse the wrath of Smokey the Bear. I trust that my new choices please the One who made the Sabbath a day of delight.

Take it from me: Choosing to pass up what a well-kept Sabbath, and Jesus, have to offer isn't too hot an idea.

18

Queen of the No-Quitters

by Trudy J. Morgan-Cole

I think we should turn back," Melanie said.

She took me by surprise. Ever since we'd started the hike, Sandi had been whining, "Can we go baaaack?" But what else would you expect from a little kid?

My friend Melanie had been on my side the whole time, going, "No, we can make it; come on!" Now Melanie had switched sides.

She checked her watch. "It took us almost an hour to get this far, and the bus is leaving in another hour," she said.

"So we've gotta keep going!" I countered. "We're more than halfway around, so it'll take us longer to go back!"

Sandi just stood there staring at us, looking exhausted. Sure, it had been a pretty rough hike. Not so bad for two eighth-graders like Melanie and me, but for a sixth-grade kid like Sandi it was tough. I wasn't sure why she had to tag along anyway.

"We know what the trail behind us is like!" Melanie pointed out to me. "But we don't know what's up ahead—it could take even longer. We're gonna get killed anyway for going off on our own. If we're not there when the bus is ready, we'll be . . . we'll be twice as killed!"

I laughed. "Look, Mel, you can see the beach from here. It's definitely closer to go on than go back. Remember, this was all your idea."

It was Melanie who had suggested we take off from a boring school picnic and go for "a little walk down by the lake." OK, so it had turned out to be more than a little walk—we'd decided to walk around the lake. And yeah, we really weren't supposed to go off on a hike without a teacher to supervise us. We were probably in for some trouble. But that was no reason to turn back.

See, I'm not a quitter. Once I start something, I always like to finish it, no matter how tough it gets. I'm very proud of that.

"Ouch! I'm up to my knees in stinging nettles!" Sandi howled from behind us.

"Look out!" Melanie cried as a tree branch whipped back and got her in the face.

"Come on! Only a little farther!" I shouted, encouraging my followers.

Just around the next bend in the shoreline I expected to see a stretch of trail that would connect us with the side of the lake where the park was—where we'd started walking a long, long time before. But when we rounded the bend, instead of the final stretch of shoreline, we faced something quite different. At this end of the lake, the water stretched way, way back in a long inlet. To walk up to the end of it and back down again might take another hour or more. Melanie was looking at her watch again.

"But we can't go back," I said. "It'd take an hour and

a half . . . we've just got to go on." I sank to the ground and put my head on my knees. This whole adventure was turning into a disaster.

Melanie looked at me on the ground and at Sandi whimpering. She took a deep breath and stepped around me, taking the lead.

"OK," she said, "you're right. For the first and only time today you're right. We've got to go on. The farther up it goes, the narrower the lake gets, and it probably gets shallower, too. We should be able to find a place where we can wade across, or maybe even swim—"

"I can't swim!" Sandi moaned.

"OK, where we can wade across," Melanie said. "Come on, let's get going."

Under the hot afternoon sun we slogged up the lakeshore, scrambling over rocks and through bushes. There was no sign of a trail now. I was afraid to ask her what time it was, but I knew it was getting close to 3:00.

Sure enough, farther up the shore the stretch of water narrowed into a river.

"This must be the river that feeds into the lake," Melanie said. "We're going to have to wade across."

The river wasn't very deep, but it sure looked fast. Golden-brown water babbled over big round stones, rushing past the banks. Sandi whined "I can't swim!" once more, just to remind us.

"You don't have to swim," Melanie said. "We can wade across. Come on, roll up your jeans."

All three of us rolled up our pant legs, took off our socks and sneakers, and got ready to cross. "We'll hold hands," Melanie decided. I was kind of glad she was making all the decisions now.

The water was so icy cold that it felt like knives stabbing our feet. And the swift-moving current made it hard to stand up. We had to pretty much drag Sandi into the water because she was so scared.

Step by step we inched across the river. It was hard to keep our footing on the smooth round stones, and every few seconds Sandi would freeze up and refuse to go any farther till we coaxed her.

"Aaaaaaagggghhh!"

The scream came from behind me at the same second I felt Sandi's hand tear loose from mine. I whipped around to see Sandi losing her balance, slipping as the rock she stood on rolled out from under her. She toppled backward, and the water rushed over her.

"Lord, don't let Sandi drown because I was a stupid idiot!" It was the quickest prayer I'd ever prayed.

Sandi's small freckled face came close to the surface, and she began to drift downstream. I lunged forward, almost losing my own footing. Then I felt her hand in mine, and as I pulled she was standing up again, sobbing and sopping wet, in front of me. There was no time to talk.

"Come on!" Melanie ordered, sounding scared.

We made it across the stream and then, dripping wet, clambered up onto the shore of the lake and started trekking back to the park. "What time is it?" I finally asked, breaking the grim silence.

"Quarter after three," Melanie replied. "Let's climb up here—we can get onto the road."

A bus full of angry and worried teachers and classmates awaited us. "You've got a lot of explaining to do when we get back to the school," our teacher warned.

"Well, I learned something today," I finally said to

Melanie when we were halfway back to town.

"Yeah?" She glared at me. "I can't wait."

"Sometimes being a quitter isn't such a bad idea—especially if you're doing something stupid in the first place."

"I couldn't agree more," she said.

19

The Mouse Experiment

by Michael J. Larson

Mr. Borman, our eighth-grade science teacher, has a slick bald head except for a narrow band of hair above his ears. His head sort of reminds me of a lightbulb.

One morning my classmates and I sat listening to Mr. "Bore-man" lecture about vacuums.

"A vacuum is a space that lacks any matter," Mr. Borman droned on. "An alarm clock ringing in a vacuum cannot be heard because there is no air to carry the sound waves."

Denny, sitting behind me, whispered, "I wish my alarm clock was in our vacuum. Then I would have an excuse for being late to school!"

"Yeah," I whispered back. "This first-period class is one I wouldn't mind being late for."

"Science is so b-o-r-i-n-g!" Denny added.

Our conversation ended abruptly as Mr. Borman spoke. "Michael and Dennis, would you care to share your discussion with us?"

We both gulped. Inside my head a voice shouted, *Ask an intelligent question . . . think of something quick!* So I sputtered the first thought that came to mind. "Mr. Borman, uh, sir, what would happen if you put a mouse in a vacuum?"

Sensing that my question might just save our hides, Denny added, "Would the mouse blow up as the pressure inside its body escaped?"

Another classmate, Sam, added, "Wow! If that happened there would be blood and guts all over!"

Several classmates cheered, while others, sympathetic to the welfare of the mouse, wailed and wept.

"Quiet!" roared Mr. Borman, and the excited voices faded.

"Dennis and Michael," began Mr. Borman, "you have asked very good questions. Perhaps someone can bring a mouse to class. We'll set up our vacuum pump and see if the mouse blows up."

Again mixtures of moans and cheers rose from my classmates. But since no one seemed to have a mouse to bring, we soon forgot the experiment, at least for that day.

As I settled into my bed that night I thought about the mouse/vacuum discussion. *If only I had a mouse!* I thought as I drifted off to sleep.

Suddenly, sitting straight up in bed, I cried, "My rabbit cage! There's a mouse nest under my rabbit cage!"

The night seemed long. I tossed and turned as I planned how I would capture the mouse.

The next morning I finished my breakfast quickly and asked my mom for an empty mayonnaise jar.

"Why, may I ask, do you want a mayonnaise jar?" she questioned, handing me the glass container.

"It's for a school project," I shouted as I bounded out the front door.

Outside I approached the rabbit cage, bent over, and lifted it slightly. "There's the nest," I whispered to myself. I moved the cage several feet away and set it down. Using a twig, I searched through the nest of shredded grass and clothing fibers. Suddenly a gray blur erupted from the nest and disappeared into the tall grass next to the cage. I grabbed the grass in my fist and came up with a squirming, wiggling mouse.

Before its sharp teeth could pierce my skin, I dropped it into the jar and secured the lid.

Won't Mr. Borman be surprised? I thought to myself with satisfaction.

When I walked into science class that morning, Mr. Borman did indeed look surprised. It seemed clear that he hadn't expected anyone to actually bring in a mouse.

Mr. Borman recovered quickly, however, and went to search the supply cabinet for the old vacuum pump. "Hope we can get this old dinosaur to work," he murmured.

Within minutes, to everyone's surprise, the ancient vacuum pump was pumping air out of a large bell jar on top of the machine.

"It works!" one student squealed with delight.

Looking at me, Mr. Borman asked, "Is the test animal ready?"

"Yes, sir," I solemnly replied.

Some classmates cheered and others groaned as I placed the frightened little animal on the pump's stand. Mr. Borman secured the thick-walled glass bell jar over the mouse. Then he turned on the vacuum pump, and slowly it began sucking air from the jar.

"I can't look!" cried one student.

Another exclaimed, "I hope there's a big explosion!"

Suddenly the mouse grew unsteady on its feet, teetered, and fell.

"The mouse fainted!" I cried.

Mr. Borman looked at me and said, "It's your mouse. Shall we shut the pump off or keep it going?"

Seeing my mouse on its back, feet quivering and seconds from death, I shouted, "Turn off the vacuum pump!"

As Mr. Borman shut off the pump, air rushed back into the bell jar.

"This mouse has suffered enough," I announced as I reached my hand under the glass bell jar to grab the helpless little creature.

The fresh air revived the unconscious rodent much quicker than I expected.

As my hand moved toward it, the mouse suddenly stood, jumped over my hand, leaped onto the table, and ran down the back of my classmate Joan.

Joan responded pretty much as anyone who had a mouse running around inside her clothing would. "Eeeeeeek!" she screamed.

The scream further frightened the mouse, and it hit the floor running. The terrified creature dashed across the science room's varnished wood floor. Since it was my mouse, I took off after it while my classmates screamed, laughed, and cheered.

The mouse headed for the open science room door with me in pursuit. Entering the long, empty hallway, the mouse suddenly had a variety of escape options.

Oh, please run to a place where I can catch you easily, I thought as I tried to keep the speeding creature in sight.

And then the unthinkable happened. The mouse ran into Mr. Melby's algebra class! Mr. Melby was also the school principal, and detentions and suspensions were all a part of his daily routine. I turned pale at this thought, but continued the chase.

As I entered the algebra classroom, the students, who had seen the mouse racing across the floor, sat momentarily stunned. Mr. Melby was frozen at the chalkboard.

Suddenly, with one great voice, the students and Mr. Melby pointed and shouted, "It went that way!"

I followed their pointing fingers to the front of the room, where a door led into an empty study hall area.

As I raced into the study hall, the not-quite-exhausted mouse was darting back and forth in the middle of the room. After several futile grabs, I finally captured the fuzzy escapee.

The science room was much calmer when I returned. I placed the mouse in the mayonnaise jar and stored it in my locker.

When the school day ended, I returned home clutching the jar with the mouse. On a farm, mice are considered harmful and worthy of destruction. But as I descended the school bus steps and walked down our driveway, I thought, *This mouse has put in quite a day. I think I'll turn it loose.*

I carried the jar behind our chicken house and dumped the perspiring, exhausted mouse on a pile of old boards. Returning to the house, I changed clothes and went outside to shoot some hoops.

I thought this story would have a happy ending, but later I saw Midnight, the family cat, crossing the yard, carrying something in her mouth.

"Oh, no!" I cried as I stood cradling the basketball

under one arm. "Midnight is about to have my research mouse for lunch!"

I'm not sure if that was my mouse. But that whole experience did get me thinking about something important.

Living without God is like living in a vacuum. We will die for sure if we don't have His love breathing life into us. The devil wants to catch each of us and watch us die, but God will keep us out of evil hands if we will let Him.

20

The Back Nine

as told to Greg Trine

Sometimes your dad says something that you know is true, but for some reason you're not paying attention. This was exactly the case when Dad told me to stay away from the back nine. In one ear and out the other.

It wasn't until later that I remembered he'd said something at all. And by then it was too late.

"See you at lunch," I called to Dad, who was taking my sister, Teri, up the bunny slope.

I got in line at chair one, which would take me to the top. From there I'd shoot over to chairs twelve and thirteen, where there would be fewer people and untouched powder—the perfect place to try out my new snowboard. I think it was then that Dad mentioned the back nine, but I was already getting on the lift and thinking about surfing the white stuff.

At the top of chair one I sat in the snow and strapped my free foot into my snowboard, then started down the hill, weaving back and forth, steering with my back foot.

The snow was nicely groomed packed powder. I wondered what the ungroomed snow would be like. And I knew the only way I'd find out would be to go to the back nine.

The back nine is the back side of the mountain. There are no lifts there, no people, no tracks in the snow. Nothing but untouched powder. It's also out-of-bounds.

Just as I expected, chair thirteen was nearly deserted. When I reached the top, I boarded over to the edge and looked down the back side. The snow was perfect. I could ski for miles. I looked over my shoulder to see if the lift operator was looking. Then I slipped over the hill out of sight . . . and into the back nine.

Wooosh. It was like floating on a cushion of air. I weaved in and out of the pines, making wide turns to keep from going too fast. *Wow,* I thought. *This sure beats the groomed stuff.*

For several minutes I descended deeper into the snow-clogged forest, giving no thought to anything but the biting wind in my face and the feel of the board beneath me. Getting back up never entered my mind.

Until I stopped.

I was pretty winded, so I sat down in the soft snow and rested. It took a while, but after I'd regained my energy, I stood up, ready to continue.

Then I looked up, and a slight twinge of fear rushed through me. Dad's warning about the back nine started replaying itself in my head. Only now I was listening.

I couldn't see the top of the hill. All around me was forest with a single track cut through the snow.

How long had I been descending? How far up was the top? Miles, maybe.

I unstrapped my board and took a step. Immediately

I sank up to my chest. In a panic I threw myself onto my back to work my feet free, then took another step. Up to my armpits in snow.

Three steps and fifteen minutes later I realized it was hopeless. I wouldn't be able to get back up, not without help. A twinge of fear shot through me again—only it wasn't just a twinge anymore. Dad wouldn't miss me for another hour, when I was to meet him for lunch. And who would know where to look? Not even the lift operator had seen me. I had made sure of it before I disappeared into the back nine.

I breathed a silent prayer: *Lord, get me home.* Then I looked hard at my situation. I had at least five hours of daylight. But it would be a while before Dad would give me up for lost and organize a search party. Right now the temperature was about twenty degrees, but after dark it would drop. If no one found me, I could freeze to death. I needed to make some kind of shelter. But before I started, I tried to see if anyone could hear me.

"Help!" I screamed at the top of my lungs. "Anyone out there?"

No answer. A soft wind blew through the pine branches. Other than that, silence. I was alone.

Using my board, I began tunneling into the snow at the base of a tree. I'd heard of people surviving severe weather conditions by tunneling. Exposed to the wind, I'd face temperatures that could easily drop below zero, especially at night. But by enclosing myself in an ice cave, I could stay alive.

I kept digging, knowing that by now Dad would be sure that I was missing. I knew he would be praying, "Lord, keep him safe. Help me find him."

It was close to three in the afternoon by the time I finished digging. Two hours of sunlight left. I called out once more, "Can anyone hear me?" No answer.

The cave was big enough to lie down in. The trunk of the tree formed one wall. Later in the day, as the sun began to fade, the wind picked up. I was glad to be protected inside.

I lay back on my board to keep myself off the cold snow. I wiggled my toes and fingers to keep the circulation going, trying to keep myself awake. But I faded into sleep anyway.

When I woke up, it was dark out. How long had I slept? My toes ached from cold. Even inside my little cave it had to be below zero.

I decided I had to keep moving if I was going to make it through the night. If I fell asleep again, I might never wake up.

I crawled out of the cave, dragging my board. In the moonlight I could see the path I had cut through the trees. If I stayed on it, maybe I'd be OK.

I placed my snowboard on the track and stomped on it, sinking into the snow. Then I picked it up and did it again. My board was my walkway through the snow. Five feet at a time I crept back up the mountain. Soon I was breathing heavily. Feeling came back to my toes. And somehow I knew that someone was praying for me—maybe many people were. I felt their strength as I moved up the hill.

Five feet at a time I kept at it, crunching my board into the snow and moving on. Hours went by. Every muscle in my body throbbed with pain. I wanted to stop, to sleep, but I fought it. *Lord, get me back.*

Finally I saw the boundary fence and the gap through which I had illegally—and foolishly—squeezed. I pulled myself to the top of chair thirteen, finally standing on hard-packed snow. Below me I saw the headlights of one of the grooming machines. I strapped into my snowboard as it neared and skied out in front of it, waving my arms and yelling, "Hey! Hey!"

A few minutes later I was sitting in the grooming machine, heading back down the mountain. The driver threw a blanket over me and announced, "A lot of people have been looking for you, young man."

"Yeah," I said thankfully. "And I'm sure a lot were praying too."

I found out later that Dad had called Mom back home, and she had started a prayer chain. I believe the power of those prayers saved my life.

Next time Dad warns me about something, I'll listen.

21

Kids in Jail

as told to Juliana Marin

Wow, cool! Hey, Lucas, let me see that!" I reached out to touch the toy gun my younger cousin Lucas was holding. "Man, this is neat. Andres, look at this! A real 09 Multi-Pistol!"

My friend Andres sauntered over and glanced at it. "Huh," he scoffed. "That little toy couldn't hit hard enough to knock a bottle down."

"It can too hit hard!" Lucas said indignantly. "Just watch!" He aimed at Andres and squeezed the trigger.

"*Yowch!*" Andres yelped. "That pellet hurt!"

I snickered, then turned back to the gun. "Whoa, if only I could show this to the guys at school."

"I'll lend it to you if you let me ride your skateboard," Lucas said eagerly.

"OK," I said.

"Santiago, are you crazy?" Andres asked. "That thing looks awfully real. If you show it at school, someone might think—"

"You worry too much. The only thing we might get in trouble for is getting there late. Those teachers are tough, you know. Come on."

I stuffed the gun into my backpack, said goodbye to Lucas, and set off for school just a few blocks away.

"Ready for the camping trip?" Andres asked.

"Yeah," I said, patting my backpack. "I've got all the clothes right here."

"Me too. I can't wait!"

My uncle Carlos, Lucas's dad, was taking me, Andres, and some cousins on a camping trip in the mountains. Colombia, where we live, has some awesome peaks. We'd leave that afternoon.

The classroom clock seemed to be broken. When the bell finally rang, I dashed out the door. "Hey, Jorge," I called to one of the guys. "Come see what I've got."

"Santiago," Andres whispered nervously, "are you sure? Maybe you should wait until we get off the school grounds."

I elbowed Andres to keep quiet and pulled the gun out. Pretty soon there was a crowd of boys around us.

"*Santiago*," Andres hissed, "one of the teachers is watching us. We might—"

"Cut it out," I said, annoyed, but I put the gun away.

"Let's go." I waved to the other guys, and we headed for home.

Andres seemed relieved now that we were away from school. "Wanna stop for a soda?" he asked as we passed by the corner store. "We have time."

"Sure," I said.

We paid for the soda and leaned against the counter. Suddenly Andres froze.

"What's wrong?" I asked.

"Santiago, did you see that guy?"

"What guy?"

"The same one who was watching us at the school."

I started to get mad. "Andres, you're paranoid. If you keep thinking that everybody is after us . . ."

Just then a police car zipped around the corner and stopped right in front of the store. Andres's eyes bugged out.

I rolled my eyes. "They're not after us. That's just . . ."

But two police officers got out of the car and walked up to us. "Excuse me, boys," one of them said gravely. "We got a report concerning two juveniles with a dangerous weapon, and we need to do a search."

"Sure," I said calmly, holding up my arms. I wasn't worried about the gun. It was a toy; anyone could see that. No problem.

The police searched us, then opened the backpacks. Slowly one of them pulled out the toy gun. Andres turned white.

"That's my little cousin's," I said casually. "It's an 09."

The officers glanced at each other. One of them pulled out a two-way radio. "Two youths caught in attempted robbery. Reporting to headquarters."

"What?" I yelped.

Suddenly one of the officers whipped me around, handcuffing my wrists behind me.

"Hey!" I shouted. "Wait a minute! That's a toy gun! How could we commit a robbery with a toy gun?"

"Most robberies by juveniles are committed with toy guns," the officer said dryly. "The victim is usually too scared to see the difference, so the kids can get away with anything."

"But there's no proof!"

The officer raised an eyebrow. "There are clothes in your backpacks. It looks as though you were planning to change afterward so you wouldn't be recognized. You may be innocent, but it doesn't seem likely."

I started to panic. The officer shoved me into the patrol car next to Andres, also handcuffed and looking sick.

"Please, mister, we're just kids," I begged. "We wouldn't rob anyone!"

One of the police officers snorted.

I stared wildly out the window as we traveled farther away from home. At the police station we were ushered through a long hallway and down the stairs to a dimly lit room. There one of the officers unhandcuffed us. I rubbed my wrists.

"Your identification papers."

Miserably I pulled them out of my wallet and handed them over. Andres did the same.

"This way."

We followed him to the end of the room, to a large metal door with a small barred window.

The color drained from my face. "Please," I croaked, "let us call home. They—"

"No talking," the officer said sharply. He shoved us into the cell, slammed the door, and locked it.

I grabbed the bars. "Wait!" I shouted.

Silence.

"Santiago," Andres said through clenched teeth, "if we ever get out of here, I'm going to kill you."

I didn't doubt it.

Andres started pacing the floor. "We've got to get out of here! Nobody will know where we are."

I nodded. Our parents might think we were with Uncle Carlos on the camping trip, and he might think we were with them. Nobody would know. We could stay in here and rot. *God, help us*, I prayed.

Time passed, maybe hours, maybe minutes.

Suddenly the door burst open. "Come on out, boys," an officer barked.

We stumbled out and followed him up the stairs, squinting in the light. He handed us our backpacks and papers.

"May we go now?" I asked in a small voice.

He nodded, and we both took off, not stopping to ask questions.

Once away from the station, Andres lost his fear and got mad. "How could they?" he shouted. "Just throw us in jail for no reason! Injustice!"

I didn't care. I was just glad to get away.

We walked for twenty minutes, Andres ranting and raving the whole way. Stopping in front of Uncle Carlos's house, Andres asked, "Do you think he'll be mad?"

I didn't have time to answer, because just then the door flew open and my uncle stormed out. "Where have you been?" he thundered. "Your parents have been worried sick, and I've driven around the neighborhood for two hours looking for you!"

"Well," I gulped, "it's a long story."

"It had better be a good one," he growled. "Go sit while I call your parents."

Soon they arrived, and after a hug from everybody, we told our story. Everyone found portions of our adventure hilarious, except for Lucas, who was mad because the police didn't return his gun.

"I'm never lending you a gun again," Lucas told me.

"Don't worry; I don't want one!" I exclaimed.

I'd had enough with guns. Sure, it was just a toy, but guns are made for killing people. Why play with something like that? Too many of us kids are getting too used to violence. We've got to stop.

Even though it took a jail cell to teach me that, I'm glad I learned.

22

Dangerous Discovery

by Gretchen Pedersen Cooper

Eyvind, wait! Don't leave for school without your ID card!" Mom frantically called. "Who knows what the Nazis will do if they discover you don't have your ID card with you!" Mom's hands shook as she handed Eyvind his card.

His blue eyes narrowed with irritation as he pulled his knit cap over his reddish-blond hair. "The Nazis are the reason for all our problems. If they hadn't invaded Denmark, Dad would still be alive."

Mom swiped her eyes as she tried to keep tears from rolling down her cheeks. "Eyvind, we can't blame everything on the Nazis. You know that your father traveled a lot for his work as a treasurer for the Seventh-day Adventist Church. He contracted malaria on a trip to Africa. The illness weakened his body—that's why he died."

"Yes, but Dad's health got worse last year on April 9, the day the Nazis invaded Denmark. Dad wouldn't have died if it wasn't for Hitler," Eyvind said as he looked down in an attempt to hide his own tears. He wanted to be strong for Mom, but some days it was just too difficult.

"Son, right now life isn't easy for any Dane. Your father always trusted God through hard times—we must do the same. Please be careful today. If you see any German soldiers, walk on the opposite side of the street," Mom instructed as she reached up to give her tall teenage son a hug.

Later in the day Eyvind glanced at the clock on the wall of the classroom. Only a few more minutes, and he would be able to forget all his troubles. He was a good student, but it was hard to sit quietly in school. There was too much time to think about all the things that made him sad.

After school Eyvind always met his friend Eric. He and Eric knew how to have fun even in difficult times.

"Where should we go today? Do you want to go to the bakery and see if there are any pastries on sale?" Eyvind asked as his stomach growled.

"That's a great idea. But first let's go down to the harbor and see if there are any new German ships," Eric suggested.

"Yeah, I—I guess we could do that," Eyvind stammered. "Mom doesn't like the idea of me going anywhere near German soldiers," Eyvind explained as he strapped his book bag on the back of his bike.

"Isn't your mom German? She shouldn't be scared of her own countrymen," Eric countered.

Eyvind frowned. "She is German. Actually, she's my stepmom, but she's the only mother I've ever known. My biological mom died when I was just a few weeks old. Dad married my stepmom when I was two years old. That's why I didn't take German classes at school. I learned German and Danish at home. Mom's nationality is German, but she is one-hundred percent against Hitler and the Nazi political party." Eyvind straightened his back as he defended his mother.

"Hey, I didn't mean anything, you know. Your mom's great," Eric nervously sputtered his apology. "I just figured she wouldn't be worried about you being around Nazi soldiers. We can skip going to the harbor today," Eric offered.

"No, let's go. I'm not scared of the Nazis. If our king, Christian, can fearlessly ride his horse in the streets of Copenhagen every day without any guards, the rest of his subjects aren't going to be afraid of the Nazis either," Eyvind retorted with conviction.

It didn't take long for the boys to reach the harbor, where the boats were docked. After parking their bikes, they took off running, looking for adventure.

Soon the boys spotted a shed. "I wonder what's inside," Eyvind said. "Hey, the door isn't locked! Let's go in!"

As the boys rushed into the shed, the door swung back, remaining only slightly ajar.

"What are these things?" Eric questioned as his eyes zoomed in on many stacks of long cylindrical objects.

"Maybe it's some kind of secret weapon," Eyvind suggested. "It's dark in here. Let's get closer and try to figure out what they are." Suddenly Eyvind's eyes widened as his hands ran over the cool metal. He whispered, "Eric, they're torpedoes! This room is full of torpedoes for German submarines!"

As their excitement turned a bit fearful, the boys ran down the rows, counting the torpedoes. Suddenly Eyvind's fast-moving feet skidded to a stop. "Eric, did you hear that sound? I think someone is coming. Quick, we've got to find a place to hide!"

The boys frantically looked around the room as the

sound of pounding feet grew closer and closer.

But it was too late. The door hit the wall as it was yanked open. A pistol held by a rigid, gloved hand met their eyes, causing the sick feeling in their stomachs to surge upward and tighten around their throats. Eric's and Eyvind's eyes traveled up from the gun to the steely gaze of a German soldier.

"Und was tust du hier?" ("What are you doing in here?") The soldier spat the words out of his mouth like the rapid firing of a machine gun.

Despite the speed of the soldier's words, Eyvind understood each and every one of them. *Help me, God,* he silently prayed. Swiftly he replied in German, *"Wir wolten nur herum."* ("We were just looking around.")

The soldier glared at the two boys. "Let me see your ID cards," he demanded.

Quickly reaching into their pockets, the boys pulled out their cards, silently transferring them from their trembling hands to the stiff, outstretched hand of the soldier.

The soldier's authoritarian, rigid posture didn't bend at all as he looked at the cards. Finally his eyes focused on the boys, studying them as if they were bugs waiting to be squashed under his heavy black boots.

Eyvind gripped the sides of his jacket, trying to still his shaking hands. Would the soldier take them straight to Nazi headquarters? What if he thought they were spies or saboteurs?

"You Danes think you can do whatever you want. It is time you realized we are here to stay," the soldier sneered. He paused, as if trying to decide what to do. "Here," he said as he slapped the cards into the boys' trembling hands. "Get out of here, and don't ever let me see you in this area again, or the two of you will be in big trouble."

Eric nodded and responded, *"Danke."* ("Thanks.")

As soon as they had cleared the door of the shed, Eyvind and Eric took off in a fast sprint, racing toward their bikes.

Finally taking a deep breath as they turned their bikes down a side street, Eyvind said, "Eric, I have never been so afraid in my life."

"I thought the soldier was going to take us straight to his headquarters," responded Eric.

"I thought the same thing," Eyvind admitted. Suddenly the weight of sadness pressing down on his shoulders seemed to lift a bit as Eyvind remembered his mom's words about trusting God.

Turning to Eric, he smiled and said, "King Christian was not here, riding by on his horse, ready to help us out of this situation. Instead, we had a stronger, greater King beside us, the King of the universe, our heavenly Father."

23

Bucketful of Trouble

by Ron Reese

Julie," called a voice from somewhere in the distance.

" 'Blessed is the one who does not walk in step with the wicked or stand in the way that sinners take . . .' "* she mumbled, trying to memorize her Bible verse from church school.

"Hey, Julie!" the voice persisted.

"Huh, what?" Julie responded as she exited study mode.

"Julie, do you want to help us give Mr. Wray a farewell gift?" Samantha asked.

"Sure, Samantha," responded Julie. "What's the gift?"

"Oh, we'll tell you all about it when we get to school." Madison winked at Samantha.

I wonder what the gift could be, Julie wondered. After the girls arrived, she found out.

"Come here," the older girls beckoned. "Here's our

---

* Psalm 1:1.

plan. First we've got to sneak into the basement of the school to get the gift."

Creeeak! Samantha eased the door to the basement open.

What's this all about? Julie kept wondering.

Finally Samantha, Madison, and Hannah returned. Whatever the gift was, it required both Madison and Hannah to carry it up the stairs. When they reached the top, Julie saw that the two girls were carrying a bucket. She dared to look inside it.

"What? You're giving Mr. Wray *water?*" Julie said, shocked.

"Shhh!" The other girls placed their forefingers to their lips. "We'll tell you about it later."

Julie followed the others out the back door and watched as Hannah climbed a ladder to the school's roof. She was followed by Madison, who stayed on the ladder near the top, and Samantha, who climbed up just a few rungs.

"OK, hand the water to me," beckoned Samantha.

Julie wasn't sure what was going on, but she knew it didn't look good. "What are you going to do with that water?" she asked.

"Shhh!" the three eighth-graders commanded Julie.

"All right, hand the bucket to me," Samantha instructed with a mischievous grin.

Against her better instincts, Julie became part of the bucket brigade.

After the others had climbed onto the roof, Samantha looked down at Julie. "Well, are you coming or not?" she asked.

Julie knew she had to be the biggest fool in the world, but she grabbed the ladder and went to find out what her friends were plotting.

When she arrived on the flat roof, Julie saw the eighth-graders moving the bucket of water toward the opposite edge of the roof.

"That way a little," Madison directed.

"No, back this way," Samantha countered.

Finally Julie could stand it no longer. She had to know what was going on. "What are you doing?" she demanded.

"This is Mr. Wray's going-away gift," Samantha said, smiling. "We're going to have him pose for a picture right below this bucket."

"Then we're going to soak him!" Madison said, giggling.

Samantha smiled sweetly. "Julie, you said you wanted to help us give Mr. Wray a going-away gift. We need you to be the one to dump the water on him."

"What?" Julie was shocked. "You want me to get your teacher wet? I would get into so much trouble!"

"No, you won't," Samantha insisted. "Besides, it's the last day of school. Nothing will happen to you."

"But what if he tells my parents?"

"We'll stand up for you," Madison said. "We'll tell them we forced you into it."

"Besides, none of us can do it," explained Samantha. "Mr. Wray is our teacher, and he'd notice if one of us was missing."

"And you're such a goody-goody that Mrs. Doral wouldn't expect you to be up to anything," Madison pointed out.

Julie hesitated. "I don't know . . ."

"Oh, come on," Samantha urged. "Do this, and you'll be our best friend!"

The offer was too good for Julie to resist. "OK. I'll do it."

The others hugged her and then arranged the plan.

Just before the school day ended, the older girls asked Mr. Wray if they could go outside for a group photo.

"That's a great idea," Mr. Wray said.

As the group passed by Julie's classroom, Samantha managed to signal to Julie that it was time for her to do her part.

"Mrs. Doral, may I use the restroom?" Julie asked. When her teacher said yes, Julie rushed past the restrooms and out the school's back door. As she raced to the ladder and climbed up, she felt bad about her actions. Mr. Wray had taught her PE and science, and he'd always been nice to her.

She could see Samantha below at the end of the sidewalk with her camera poised as if she were going to take a picture.

"OK, Mr. Wray, can you get between Daniel and Stephen?" Samantha requested.

From above, Julie could see that their teacher was now positioned directly beneath the pail of water.

Julie waited for the signal.

"OK, everyone looks great," Samantha said, smiling. "But we'd better hurry, because it looks like rain!"

"Rain" was the signal Julie had been listening for. She tipped the bucket over and held onto it so that only the water would plummet toward the teacher below.

"*Arrrggghhh!*" Mr. Wray shrieked.

"Bull's-eye!" shouted Samantha.

Julie couldn't believe how well their plan had worked. The teacher was drenched! She couldn't help smiling as Mr. Wray looked upward to find the source of the sudden "downpour." As he did, Julie noticed that he wasn't smiling.

"Julie Bates, come down off that roof this instant!" Mr. Wray shouted.

Quickly Julie ran back inside.

"Julie," called Mr. Wray, "come here this instant!"

She'd never seen the teacher act this way. It suddenly occurred to her that this was one of the stupidest things she'd ever done. Fearful, she crawled underneath her teacher's desk.

"Julie, what's going on?" asked Mrs. Doral.

Julie now saw Mr. Wray's soggy form enter and stand next to the desk, dripping water on the floor.

"Um, I dumped a bucket of water on Mr. Wray." She softly added, "I—I'm sorry, Mr. Wray."

There was a long pause. Then Mr. Wray said, "Thank you for the apology, Julie. I was just really worried when I saw you up on top of the roof."

"Um, am I in trouble?" she asked.

"Well, you've said you're sorry, and I'm pretty sure you really meant it. That's enough."

As she thought about the teacher's kind attitude, Julie felt tears sliding down her cheeks. She truly felt sorry for what she had done. She knew that what her friends had planned was wrong, but she had done what they said even though she knew better. *Next time I'll be stronger*, she determined in her heart. *With God's help, I won't let anybody convince me to do something that's wrong.*

That night Julie shared with her father what she'd been involved with that day. Her father called the other parents, who had already heard about the incident. Each girl then had to do what Julie had already done—apologize to their teacher. Four girls would make much wiser choices in the future!

Guide's Greatest Stories
THE BEST OF THE BEST

From change of heart stories to hero stories, from angel stories to mystery stories, the Guide's Greatest series has invaluable character-building stories for the juniors, earliteens, and teens in your life! These true stories from the pages of *Guide* magazine will keep kids (and their parents) inspired and entertained!

Collect them all

- ❑ Guide's Greatest Hope Stories
- ❑ Guide's Greatest Discovery Stories
- ❑ Guide's Greatest Friendship Stories
- ❑ Guide's Greatest Narrow Escape Stories
- ❑ Guide's Greatest Prayer Stories
- ❑ Guide's Greatest Mission Stories
- ❑ Guide's Greatest Angel Stories
- ❑ Guide's Greatest Christmas Stories
- ❑ Guide's Greatest Sabbath Stories
- ❑ Guide's Greatest Mystery Stories
- ❑ Guide's Greatest Funny Stories
- ❑ Guide's Greatest Miracle Stories
- ❑ Guide's Greatest Faith Stories
- ❑ Guide's Greatest Animal Stories
- ❑ Guide's Greatest Change of Heart Stories
- ❑ Guide's Greatest Grace Stories
- ❑ Guide's Greatest Escape From Crime Stories
- ❑ Guide's Greatest Hero Stories

HEY KIDS! Check out our cool games and puzzles
www.pacificpress.com/games

Pacific Press
PUBLISHING ASSOCIATION

AdventistBookCenter.co

AdventistBookCenter

@AdventistBooks

YouTube AdventistBooks

eBooks are available a
Adventist-eBooks.com

3 WAYS TO ORDER: **1**– Adventist Book Center® **2**– 1-800-765-6955 **3**– AdventistBookCenter.co